AFRICA'S PATH TO ECONOMIC DEVELOPMENT

.

AFRICA'S PATH TO ECONOMIC DEVELOPMENT

A Guide For Policy Makers and Scholars

Joseph S. Fomunung

Spears Media Press
DENVER
www.spearsmedia.com

Spears Media Press LLC
DENVER
7830 W. Alameda Ave, Suite 103-247 Denver, CO 80226
United States of America

First Published in 2018 by Spears Media Press
www.spearsmedia.com
info@spearsmedia.com
Information on this title: www.spearsmedia.com/product/Africas-path

Ordering Information:
Special discounts are available on bulk purchases by corporations, associations, and
others. For details, contact the publisher at any of the addresses above.

ISBN: 9781942876267 (Paperback)
Also available in Kindle (ebook)

Book & Cover Design by Spears Media Press
Cover Photograph: (CCO) Pexels.com

*To the fallen Founding Fathers of the Organization of African Unity,
which has since morphed into the African Union*

&

*To the memories of my late parents, Prince Gabriel Ningmua Fomunung
and Queen Elizabeth S. Kayeba Fomunung, who saw and carried out the
needed sacrifices to ensure that I, along with all my siblings, received the
best education that their modest finances could afford.*

Contents

ACKNOWLEDGEMENTS

For a very long time following the completion of my formal graduate school education, I always envisioned myself writing a book that would serve as a guide for decision-makers for a united strong and developed Africa. It took this long to realize this work because I was overtaken by the need to raise a family, whom I subsequently transplanted across two continents to settle in the United States. However, were it not for a few diehard encouragers and individuals who believed in my capability to produce this kind of work, it would have remained a pipe dream. These academics in their own right are researchers, chairs and department heads in their various universities.

Over the years, they were avid readers of my many articles on development and related subjects, and suggested that I produce, in their own words, "A Compendium of Papers" consisting of all my articles written in various journals and media. Principal among these intellectuals and academics are US-based Dr. Jerry K. Domatob, Dr. Victor Gomia, Dr. Kehbuma Langmia and my young friend, Dr. Pascal Doh in Finland. Another towering academic Dr. Jude Fokwang is the one who did the final editing and suggested formatting that would meet high academic standards as well as the publisher's requirements for this type of academic work. These are the gentlemen, among many other unnamed, who encouraged and urged me on over a two-decade period to write a book. Without their encouraging words and belief in me, this book would not be possible. To each of you, I say, Thank You.

I was also encouraged by two renowned Cameroonian journalists and editors-in-chief of the Cameroon national daily *Cameroon Tribune,* namely Mr. Richard Nyamboli and Mr. Shey Peter Mabuh. They would edit some of my acerbic articles from time to time to protect me from the censors and enforcers who guarded the not-so-tolerant system. In retrospect, I really do appreciate their actions which largely left the core of my messages intact. To these two men of words, accept my profuse thanks for your professionalism and concern for my safety.

Furthermore, I would also like to acknowledge the patience demonstrated by my beautiful wife and partner, Theresa A. Fomunung, for taking in stride my antics. Once I sat on the computer writing this book, I would ignore her presence as this took precedence over all else for hours in the stretch. I cannot thank her enough for allowing me the needed space to work on this book. It takes understanding by one's partner to achieve this kind of mind focused work. Thank you, my love.

Last but not least, is a young gentleman—a published author in his own right with four books including a trilogy to his name on Amazon. An author and wordsmith, MBA from HULT International Business School, as well as an entrepreneur, this young man is responsible for having goaded me to finally sit down and write this book. His persistence for me to, as he would always put it, "Put your learned mind to help people by writing a book on development" is what finally got me onto the computer. This young man happens to be one of my sons—Kenneth S. Fomunung a.k.a. Kennyrich. Not only did he give me that final nudge but took precious time to edit the entire book. No one was better placed than someone who has written and published four books. Thank you very much, son, for your confidence in my abilities and assistance editing this book. You made it happen. In no small measure, all my children, including the physician Dr. Edmond Fomunung also took interest in, and encouraged me to put my experiences and humanity in book form that would benefit others.

INTRODUCTION

Africa is a vast continental landmass, second in size only to Asia. A continent of about 30 million square kilometers with a population of approximately 1.2 billion people, 55 countries make up the continent, speaking around 2,000 languages.

According to the World Bank and the Organization for Economic Co-operation and Development (OECD), over the past decade, six of the world's ten fastest growing economies are in Africa. These include Kenya, Cote d'Ivoire, Rwanda, Ethiopia, Tanzania, and Senegal. Nigeria, Ghana, Mozambique and South Africa did not make the top ten fastest growing African economies according to 2015 IMF/WBG rankings, even though they remain among the top countries with a favorable perception rating for doing business in.

More than half of Africa's population is between ages 15 and 24, and its average GDP growth has been hovering around 5% annually. This is almost double the world average of 2.6%. Its politics are as diverse as its geography and its cultures. The contrasts are enormous as the continent has about twenty countries with GDP of $2,000 USD and below, with ten at GDP per capita of $3,000 plus.

Today, only Equatorial Guinea has a GDP per capita of $33,000 USD, comparable to many European countries. Libya was the only other country with a high per capita GDP before NATO's ill-advised intervention that toppled Muammar Gaddafi and killed him in 2011. Gabon is another country with a GDP of $17,230 USD (2013).

Even though Africa's water resources are three times its landmass, up to 358 million lack access to potable water. Despite having 40% of the world's biodiversity and 60% of the world's arable land, Africa has been a net importer of food since the 1970s to sustain its burgeoning population, which is projected to reach 2 billion by 2030, half of whom would be in the labor force.

It is obvious then, that this huge army of unemployed, but employable population would pose challenges for policy makers and development practitioners. The middle class is growing, and consumers are becoming more sophisticated and discerning. The youth are a teeming segment, expecting and demanding greater voice on policy formulation and policy implementation. They are more interconnected via internet and social media and are more computer and business savvy than the older generation. As a result, African policy makers would have no choice but to create space for them as important stakeholders.

Moreover, more African countries are prioritizing value added through transformational activities of raw materials and moving away from purely commodity producers and exporters. In 2004, investment in extractive industries—natural resources—accounted for 25% of all FDI projects in Africa. In 2013, this proportion was only 5%.

By contrast, retail and consumer products accounted for the second largest of FDI projects, making up 17% of all projects in Africa. Most countries still depend on commodities export for foreign exchange revenue. The prices have declined within the past decade, consequently straining state budgets. Governments are hard pressed to provide basic needs while servicing international loans.

These are the problems and challenges that Africa is facing and is likely to continue facing as its leaders take a resolute route to economic and political integration. This book, therefore, is an attempt to further identify and analyze the forces and actors that would shape the continent going forward and propose recommendations to policy makers and development practitioners in meeting these challenges.

Unlike other works on the subject of the motherland, this book deliberately calls out Africa's political leaders to open up and create room for other stakeholders, but particularly, to build strong national and continental institutions that would outlast office holders. It also calls on political leadership to craft institutions that allow for altering power by establishing and respecting term limits. They are reminded that they should be ephemeral while national and continental institutions should be more permanent. Recent developments in a growing number of African countries however, point disappointingly to the reverse- leaders amending their countries' constitutions to eliminate term limits. This trend does not augur well for the future hopes and expectations of the younger generations waiting in the wings to take over the reins of leadership and redirect continental development differently from the drift that has kept it lagging behind other world regions for far too long.

This overarching theme shall be seen repeatedly as we examine the daunting task of creating an Africa that is robust economically and independent politically, with a common market, one parliamentary institution with a single currency and its own central bank to control and regulate its economy.

List of Abbreviations

AU	African Union
EY	Ernst & Young
IMF	International Monetary Fund
OECD	Organization of Economic Cooperation and Development
IFF	Illicit Financial Flow
FDI	Foreign Direct Investment
DRC	Democratic Republic of Congo
EAC	East African Community
ECCAS	Economic Community of Central African States
COMESA	Common Market for Eastern and Southern Africa
NEPAD	New Partnership for Africa's Development
MNC	Multinational Corporation
SADC	Southern African Development Community
STEM	Science Technology Engineering Mathematics
TNC	Transnational Corporation
TFTA	Tripartite Free Trade Area
UN	United Nations
UNDP	United Nations Development Program
UNECA	United Nations Economic Commission for Africa
UNCTAD	United Nations Conference on Trade and Development
UNFAO	United Nations FOOD and Agricultural Organization
UNFCCC	United Nations Framework Conference on Climate Change
UNESCO	United Nations Educational and Scientific Organization
WB	World Bank
WBG	World Bank Group
WTO	World Trade Organization
WHO	World Health Organization

CHAPTER ONE

INCEPTION

Tackling or even attempting to write suggestively on what could be the best path to Africa's economic development is like looking for a needle in a haystack. This situation is underscored by the countless publications that economists, political economists, political scientists and numerous development experts have published.

Innumerable approaches spanning more than five decades have seen the light of day, yet Africa still lags behind the rest of the world in just about every facet and index of social and economic development. Added to this task has been the conundrum of prescribing solutions to a continental grouping of about 55 countries with a multiplicity of languages and subcultures that range from indigenous African languages and cultures to European, Arabic as well as other subcultures.

Africa is one huge landmass that best describes the term geographic diversity—itself being at once a hindrance as well as a facilitator of economic development. Daunting would be an understatement to analyzing politically, economically and culturally, a continent that can absorb at least three other continents and a host of other countries. Experts have tried to various degrees of success. These experts have come from Europe, the Americas and Africa.

While there's no gainsaying that most proponents on this vexatious perennial problem have come from, and followed the Western economic development model, it was not until fairly recently—within the last three decades—that economists and development practitioners of African origin, whether based in Africa or in the diaspora, began challenging some core assumptions, tenets and premises upon which Western development experts and scholars had based their recommendations bilaterally and multilaterally.

Most of the recommendations advanced so far by scholars of

Africa's developmental challenges have been subsumed in content and form under categorizations that fall short of other key Africa-specific factors. I shall try to be as perspicacious as possible in approaching these problems while remaining cognizant of my own intellectual and other limitations. To claim to be complete or pretend to exhaustively offer the solutions to Africa's developmental woes would be fallacious and dishonest at best.

For simplicity and clarity, this book shall, by necessity, be approached from a political economic perspective. The advantages of this approach cannot be overemphasized for the following reasons:

- Past publications have repeatedly failed to take into consideration the specificities of Africa and by extension, the diversity of the countries that make up the vast continent.
- The existing and lingering vestiges and legacies of colonialism.
- The international political system wherein supranational institutions like the United Nations and its ancillary organizations such as the World Bank and International Monetary Fund, and their private funding arm-the International Finance Corporation, play preponderant roles in shaping the direction of policy decisions in almost all African countries.

Approaching the continent's developmental challenges from the political economic perspective permits one to be more holistic, coalescing and flexible.

If we proceed from the undeniable premise that each nation state constantly seeks to identify, explore, exploit opportunities to enhance its citizens' wellbeing and protect its national interests, then it goes without doubt that the more powerful players would repeatedly pursue those interests to the detriment of weaker state actors. This being the case, the weaker states would almost perpetually find themselves at the shorter end of the world economic spectrum since the system would be largely negatively skewed against them.

Today, as has been for over five decades, it goes without saying, therefore, that the current international system is inherently conflictual since it is based on, and prone to inequality—a condition that has been identified as a source of disputes and conflicts intranationally and internationally.

It would take the concerted efforts of all global players to demonstrate the deliberate willingness to fairness. Thus, the onus, I contend, would be on more powerful stakeholder members of the international community to share and show restraint in consumption to begin to reverse these unacceptable imbalances.

For Africa to develop socioeconomically, a conscious and conscientious paradigm shift would have to take place. This, I believe, is where the greatest difficulty lies. We are essentially asking developed nations whose wealth can be partially traced to the past and ongoing exploitation of the Africa's natural resources to scale down their rate of consumption of the world's resources. Their way of life would not change, nor their standard of living decline. Anything less would not address Africa's perennial problems of underdevelopment given the globalized and interdependent nature of the world economy.

An operational definition of some key concepts upon which this book shall be based are examined below. Since economic development necessarily has to be directed by government, whose policy decisions impinges on individual, group and company decision making—following government's monetary and fiscal policies, we shall posit here a definition of Political Economy.

Political Economy has been variously defined, but for the purposes of this book, I shall define political economy as the study and use of how economic theory and methods influence political ideology. Political economy is, therefore, the interplay between economics, law and politics and how policy decisions emanate therefrom.

Put differently, it is the study of the interrelationships of political policies and economic processes and their influences on social institutions as a unified subject. It studies how institutions develop in different social and economic systems and how public policies are developed and implemented.

What makes political economy a complex subject is its inherently built competing interests between individuals and groups on how best to develop a country's economy—with finite resources dictating policies. Note must be made here that no economic system efficiently distributes resources, as that system would have Pareto Efficiency or Optimality.

Pareto Efficiency assumes that a country's resources are so efficiently distributed that any party's interests cannot be satisfied without denying other parties the same resources. In practice, such an economic system does not exist, whether it be in the Capitalist, Socialist, Communist or Communalist systems.

It is my view that every economic system has a component of

each system. Government remains the principal actor and driver of every economic system, directing growth through a combination of instruments regardless of whether its system is the five-year planned development common in Communism, or the "free" market of Capitalism. There is, therefore, no completely free, unbridled private economic system in existence.

In capitalist systems, the government creates the enabling environment by putting in place legal frameworks within which private enterprise functions. In communist and socialist systems, the government has a more hands-on approach in directing key economic sectors. In all systems, the government has the responsibility to build the core infrastructure upon which economic activities would be based and grow. These are reasons why the aforementioned Political Economy is important.

Economic Development

The concept of economic development is one of those overused, misused and abused terms that almost every scholar and non-scholars alike lay claim as to its meaning. While each may have some general knowledge as to its true meaning, it is that one field that developed into a profession without many realizing it. I shall make an attempt here to encompass what I hope would serve as an operational understanding of this important concept.

Economic development may be seen as the scope that includes the process and policies by which a nation improves the economic and social wellbeing of its citizens. It incorporates literacy rates, life expectancy and poverty rates. Health and education are equally factors of economic development.

Since economic development sets out to raise a people's wellbeing, it must necessarily involve economic growth, which concerns itself with productivity and rise in GDP or aggregate output of goods and services. Thus, economic growth can be seen as just one aspect of economic development.

The practitioners of economic development have two key roles: one is to provide leadership in policy formulation, and the other is to administer policy, programs and projects. In many African countries, poor policy frameworks and policy formulations have been identified as weak and flawed. Nevertheless, a few have had great policy frameworks and demonstrated progress and could serve as useful examples going forward.

The second role—execution or administering policy decisions—is problematic, as factors that enter into designating the administrators or executors are where outcomes have been directly linked to the success or failure of policy decisions designed to foster economic development. When centrifugal forces, notably tribalism and nepotism, become important factors in designating individuals as administrators, the satisfactory results of development programs and projects become in doubt.

The tribal factor, in particular, has been the greatest Achilles' heel that has killed programs and projects in many African countries, as those so designated are usually not chosen from a pool of competent individuals, but largely from tribal groupings by the tribe at the helm of statecraft at the time. When this happens, the results are cost overruns, scandalous and costly delays caused by corruption, waste, abuse and loss of natural and scarce financial resources.

According to United Nations statistics, for some very corrupt African nations, approximately $10 billion to $20 billion USD of national budgets leave the economy for offshore private accounts. Africa loses up to $50 billion annually via illicit financial outflows[1] Furthemore, according to the Global Financial Integrity 2017 report and the IMF Directorate of Trade Statistics, some US$854 billion left Sub Saharan Africa over a 39 year period accounting for between 7.5% and 11.6% of total trade.[2] This practice - illicit financial outflows, while not being overtly encouraged by recipient country financial institutions, is nonetheless responsible when they and their governments turn a blind eye to these illegal fund transfers. As a former Political Economics professor of this author once said, "These stolen funds by Third World politicians and administrators make available cheap money for businesses in developed nations for investments."

Administration versus Management

I believe that the line between the concepts of Administration and Management are not that thin as some have maintained. Understanding the differences is of paramount importance in the African context, in formulating policies and making macroeconomic decisions. I believe that this goes back to the negative legacies left by the former European colonial powers wherein administrators were trained to ensure colonial interests were maintained, protected and promoted.

Consequently, the indigenous peoples were never taught management or managerial skills as we know today, to the effect that after independence, which was clearly limited to political, the economies of these so called independent states were left wanting in managerial efficiency. That state of affairs has had lasting ramifications to this day and has permeated every sector of modern day African society.

This situation carried over to the institutions that came out of the former colonies with devastating effects. France, for example, built schools of administration through which administrative functionaries were trained to handle administrative functions. I believe that there are important differences between one who is managing a for-profit-company, a government or public office, and an organization.

Even though each might have similar goals of employing resources efficiently to attain desired outcomes, the manager of a business company would not employ same resources in material, human and time as his counterpart would in managing a government ministerial department. Similarly, a manager of an NGO would have different priorities than a manager of a for-profit enterprise.

An enterprise manager, for example, would, when given charge of a company, put into place such departments or divisions as R&D, marketing, including market research/analysis to know the competition, and finance, accounting and forecasting. Expanding the bottom line through growth promotion strategies to satisfy the shareholders and ensuring dividend increases would be his or her priorities. So, naturally, the kind of talent search and recruitment from competing pools of qualified professionals and experts would differ from the types of talents needed for a public organization.

However, the same cannot be said of one in charge of a government ministerial department or an NGO. This situation is troublesome since these administrators are generally trained in public administration, which has a curriculum that is conspicuously devoid of management expertise and other managerial traits suited for private enterprise. A case in point is the grouping of former French colonies in Africa, who are appointed to manage parastatal or para public for-profit corporations.

There is a prevailing belief that once appointed to manage these corporations, these individuals, hired solely or primarily because of their association with the powers that be or key decision-makers, become entitled to siphon off development investment funds for personal use while singing praises to the man in power. This phenomenon is commonplace in many African countries. Professor George Ayittey the Ghanaian economist put it best when he stated "African government officials do not serve the people. The African state has been reduced to a mafia-like bazaar, where anyone with an official designation can pillage at will. In effect, it is a state that has been hijacked by gangsters, crooks and scoundrels. They have seized and monopolized both political and economic power to advance their own selfish agenda and criminal activities, not to develop their economies."[3]

Their overarching obsession is to amass personal wealth, gaudily displayed in flashy automobiles, fabulous mansions and a bevy of fawning women. Helping the poor, promoting economic growth or improving the living standard of their people is anathema to the ruling elites. Faithful only to their foreign bank accounts, these official buccaneers have no sense of morality, justice or even patriotism. They would kill, maim, torture and even destroy their own countries to acquire and protect their booty because as functional illiterates, they are incapable of using whatever knowledge they acquired from education to get rich on their own in the private sector. Sadly, French speaking Africa south of the Sahara grouped into the Francophonie are at the helm of affairs at all these fourteen countries trained in the French set up colonial schools of Administration and Magistracy. The most notable feature of these institutions is they admit the most well connected not the academically brilliant.

By contrast, under normal, merit-based hiring circumstances, a corporation would bring in a qualified CEO or General Manager who has the attributes of a good and efficient manager capable of carrying out R&D for improved products and services, conducting market studies and developing a strategy to grow and expand business. These new managers of modernization would gladly employ such managerial tools as SWOT, PEST and SVOR for projects and programs. Expansion would normally absorb the unemployed, thus expanding the tax base and leading to further economic growth.

However, most of these presidential decree-appointed tribesmen with guaranteed salaries are under no pressure to practice efficient management, and this single factor has been known to account for the failure of many of these for-profit corporations in Africa. Even in cases where one finds a competent, results- oriented General Manager, he does not usually have free rein to manage because periodically, he or she must send part of the company profits, or worse still, a portion of its investment budget, to the politicians in the capital city.

As if that unusual item missing from the company's income statement or any other legitimate financial records was not enough drain on misdirected financial resources, the local political and administrative cadres within whose jurisdiction the corporation is located and operating not only expect but demand their own share as well.

What we see here is a revolving door phenomenon wherein the GM's longevity at the helm of a development program or project depends on factors far removed from objective, efficient and satisfactory results and evaluation. In stark contrast, in a normal and traditional business enterprise, a GM's tenure at the helm of such a corporation would depend largely on him or her delivering a stellar performance, satisfying Key Performance Indicators (KPI's), driving growth and ensuring profitability of that business, since shareholders would expect increasing dividends over time.

It is important to note that recent trends in some parts of the world have shown that not all economic growth leads to economic development. Development practitioners have increasingly begun questioning long held theories about how economic growth is linked to economic development. Quite a handful of African countries have experienced this phenomenon and debate is ongoing to determine why such is the reality on the African continent, whereas East Asian countries showed both growth and development with increased per capita income during that region's economic transformation.

Macroeconomics

One cannot fully understand political economy without getting a handle on Macroeconomics. Simply stated, macroeconomics deals with price increases and decreases. It looks at the economy holistically. Macroeconomists help forecast economic conditions to help consumers, companies and governments make better decisions.

When the price of a product rises, it may be due to scarcity of raw materials used in the production of that product or some interruption in distribution such as war or inclement weather. It could also result from price fixing by producers such as a cartel, or by using technological advantages intra-nationally and internationally thus affecting price structure via trade.

Macroeconomics helps us understand a nation's economic behavior as opposed to microeconomics, which deals with individuals and groups and their behaviors within any given economy. Macroeconomics helps us understand:

- How consumers are interested in employment opportunities, costs of goods and services and cost of borrowing money.
- How companies and businesses use macroeconomic analysis to determine expansion of production or contraction. If they feel more money will be available, they will expand and employ more workers and vice versa.
- How governments use macroeconomic analysis to budget for investment and spending, creating taxes, deciding interest rates and making policy decisions.

National Output: Gross Domestic Product

Gross Domestic Product (GDP) refers to the total amount of goods and services a country produces. As a snapshot of the economy at a certain period of time, GDP helps explain macroeconomics as it uses real GDP factoring in inflation as opposed to nominal GDP, which reflects only changes in prices. The nominal GDP figures will be higher if inflation rises from year to year, so it is not necessarily indicative of output levels from the entire economy, only higher prices.

GDP can be considered a stepping stone into macroeconomic analysis. Government policies can and do trigger economic cycles that alternate between recessions and booms. Government policies do also trigger consumer behavior as in taxation or some international phenomenon. Based on the past, macroeconomists attempt to forecast the future performance of the whole national economy. These predictions can be done with whole world regions as well.

Inflation

Inflation is the rate at which prices of goods and services rise in an economy. Consumer Price Index (CPI) measures the current prices of a selected basket of goods and services at a given period. Whenever nominal GDP is higher than real GDP, we can assume that the prices of goods and services have been rising. Ideally, demand is supposed to determine supply or production levels.

Occasionally, however, supply side economics can be deliberately triggered by government to spur demand by increasing supply. President Reagan was a disciple of supply side economics and his economic policies led to deficit spending and increased national debt in the US economy, since defense outlays ballooned under his administration. In order to feed demand and supply, government has to print money and inject it into the economy via the country's Central Bank.

Greasing the Economic Engine—Role of Government

Monetary Policy

When there is a need to increase the money supply in an economy, the central bank will buy government bonds, which will result in monetary expansion. This government action will reduce the cost of borrowing money and the reduced cost will spur and expand production of goods and services as more people would be employed by the increased investments by businesses. Demand will rise and further expand output levels.

However, in a country where a large percentage of goods and services are not produced locally, but instead imported, the picture would be different, and results would vary. This situation is an indication of unfavorable balance of payment from international trade as it means more is being imported than produced and exported. The only small benefit might come from that portion of the population that have found more employment opportunities in the service sector, but the local economy would not be capable of absorbing the local unemployed were those goods to be manufactured locally.

Conversely, when the central bank wants to contract the economy, it will sell off treasury bonds and this action will result in a rise in interest rates, rendering the cost of borrowing money more expensive. With reduced money supply in circulation, reduced spending by government and consumers, demand will be depressed, and prices will lead to lower output.

Fiscal Policy

Government can raise taxes or lower government spending and trigger contraction. If it does either, the economy will produce less output. On the other hand, to achieve a fiscal expansion, the government decreases taxes or increases spending. Either way, a rise in real output will occur due to more disposable income being available to individuals and businesses in the population.

Economic Distortions and the Dilemma

Now that we have a pretty good understanding of key economic terms in an economy, we shall now turn to examining some fundamental questions as to how these concepts operate in the economies of African countries. This is particularly important, given that lots of major economic decisions are not sovereignly taken by national leaders, but are influenced by outside decision-makers, multilaterally and bilaterally, thus distorting the entire economic landscapes.

This quagmire is even more glaring in countries that are former French colonies, where two groupings of countries use the French printed currency - CFA francs, pegged to a currency that no longer exists, and where none of these groupings of countries has the power of, nor plays the traditional roles that central banks play in both monetary and fiscal policies to regulate the economy. How these basic economic concepts operate in these African countries remains a quandary, and that is if at all they work.

The Current International System

One does not need to be a genius to see that there are many flaws with the current international system that the entire world economy has been built upon and has been operating within for more than a century. This system became strengthened and more pronounced following the end of World War II as the United Nations succeeded the old League of Nations, and as many former colonies of European countries began agitating for their independence.

As the saying goes, "Freedom is seldom accorded on a silver

platter without loss of lives or without blood, tears and sweat." Naturally, there was resistance on the part of the colonial masters to relinquish power to those clamoring for independence as evidenced by the resultant bloody wars that would eventually culminate in the late 1950s and early 1960s in these colonies gaining their political independence.

However, independence was not granted without strangulating strings attached in many of the new African nations, and this is even truer regarding the former French colonies of Africa, who to this day, still maintain close cultural, economic, political and military ties to Paris. These ties, more or less imposed on the African ex-colonies by France before independence, were a conspicuous condition for such independence.

Today, as has been the case since the 1960s, up to fourteen African countries still pay a colonial tax to the French treasury, and none of these fourteen prints its own currency. Since 1960, this situation has taken away the role that each sovereign nation's central bank is expected to play in monetary and fiscal policy of regulating and controlling the national economy. Exacerbating French speaking Africa's economies are some confounding binding protocols that obliges all fourteen former French colonies to keep up to 50 percent of their foreign exchange reserves in the French national treasury. Furthermore, these funds are borrowed at a whopping fifteen percent rate of interest. These are some of the reasons that account for the relative underdevelopment of much of Francophone Africa. The OECD and some Nordic countries opposed to these ongoing French policies estimate that upward of $500 billion or €440 billion leaves Africa annually to keep France's economy among the developed world group of countries. It is safe to state that French-speaking Africa would continue to lag behind her English-speaking sister countries unless or until these strangulating imposed treaties and protocols are relaxed or eliminated. The existence of these ties begs the question of how independent the French-speaking African countries are.

When the decision to determine a country's domestic money supply is in the hands of a foreign nation as is the case with these African countries who have France in such a role, the national economy only functions at the mercy of that entity wielding power over the currency, hitherto France. To illustrate the significance and gravity of this unfortunate state of affairs hogtying the sovereignty of so-called independent African nations that are former French colonies, allow me to share these words by Jacob Rothschild, of the famed or infamous Rothschild dynasty: "Give me control of a nation's currency and I wouldn't care who runs its politics."[4]

It is therefore evident that this state of affairs - monetary imperialism has far reaching ramifications with respect to the autonomy of the governments and the wellbeing of the people of these countries.

CHAPTER TWO

GOVERNANCE AND INSTITUTIONS

In this chapter, we will examine two principal forms of institutions that are prevalent in many African countries, and which have shaped and been shaped by history. These are indigenous and exogenous institutional types. These represent important players in the Africa we find today, the Africa that has been labeled the 'Dark Continent,' the Africa portrayed in the West on television screens as plagued with diseases, war, famine and misery.

African nations are rather unique on a set of important national development issues nonetheless. A marked characteristic of most African governments is the presence of very strong men at the helm of statecraft and a corresponding absence of strong national institutions. This is a carryover of the governance type from the colonial era and has endured, in one form or another, to varying degrees in most countries that make up the African continent.

Indigenous Institutions

Before the arrival of Europeans in Africa, traditional governing institutions existed and flourished well under kings, and societies were in harmony, living in communal systems. While the old powerful empires and kingdoms of Gao, Songhai, Timbuktu and Ashanti went into the history books, smaller kingdoms survived.

These kingdoms have survived the modern governance systems till this day, albeit diminished in authority and relevance. Most African nations have existing traditional kingdoms called fondoms, chiefdoms, emirs, sultanates or lamidos, depending on the countries being examined or the region within these countries.

These traditional kingdoms thrive side-by-side with modern governmental structures. While in some countries, these kingdoms have been respected, heeled and kept as auxiliaries of the modern administrative governmental apparatus, in other countries, the relationship between the two systems have not been particularly harmonious, leading to occasional tensions as to who should have greater authority over the populations and jurisdictions of ethnic and ethnolinguistic entities.

Largely though, most modern African governments have worked out the type of arrangement that mutually recognizes each other's authority as long as the traditional kings recognize the national government's role over the entire national territory in matters of overall national development plans, defense, foreign policy and monetary policies.

Today, stark differences exist between those African countries that were colonized by Britain and those that were colonized by France. While the British largely encouraged and left more local decision making to the colonized people, France on the other hand, preferred an assimilationist policy with a strong presence and a firm hand in the administration of all levels and sectors in the colonies.

The French gave the illusion to a few select trained individuals that they were equal to their colonial masters by allowing them to sit in sessions at the French National Assembly, for example. The French forced the abandonment of native cultures and traditional wears by local kings, providing alternate French-designed uniforms and making these kings subordinate to Paris-appointed District Officers called *Sous Préfets* and *Préfets*. London, on the other hand, ruled through local structures known as Native Authorities.

The implications of the French colonial policy were and is as it is said, "Lose your culture and you lose your identity," and it has not been helpful. Today, the legacy of this French colonization style is visible across the world, but particularly, in Africa. For example, most ex-French colonial nations would not take independent decisions at the United Nations voting without first consulting Paris. The good news is that this may be changing as the new generation of Africans are awakening and challenging this neocolonial mindset and practice. They do not feel bound by these outdated practices and debilitating neocolonial bonds.

One factor that economic developers from the West have failed to notice is the linkages that exist between the traditional African kingdom style of governance and the modern system. In former

French African nations, Paris used the local kingdom structures, wherein the kings wielded near unquestionable power over their populations, to assimilate them into the modern governance, counting on and basing their nation's stability on the tradition of villagers following their kings, fons, chiefs, lamidos or sultans. Following independence, it is evident that this policy has worked to the benefit of the neocolonial power, France, to this day.

One casualty of this system has been the proclivity to centralize power by the national elite sitting in the national capital cities. Unlike in France, where there is some form of checks and balances despite having a strong presidential system, the same was deliberately not encouraged in the colonies, and democracy suffered as a consequence. The strong presidential system of government meant that too much power was concentrated in the executive without any countervailing powers.

Concentration and centralization created a fertile breeding ground for corruption, nepotism, a muzzled press and a weakened private sector. I posit here that the existing systems as practiced since the 1960s have contributed to the misallocation of resources and the resultant underdevelopment of many African countries, especially ex-French colonies, to this day.

It is equally safe to maintain that the existence of strong presidential systems in Africa, with all their inherently built corruption, lethargy, nepotism plus human and natural resources misallocation, stands out as one of the key causes of social and economic underdevelopment in the continent. Jobs and lofty government positions as well as access to government contracts are usually not awarded based on experience and expertise to do the job, but on the degree or intensity of political affiliation or tribal belonging. Some contracts are only awarded to businesses whose bosses have either promised a healthy chunk of money or have actually effected these under-the-table acts. The results become shoddy jobs, inefficiently executed projects whose life cycles are often very short-lived.

These poorly executed, underfunded projects end up costing taxpayers huge sums of money. The term 'taxpayer money' is a foreign concept in most African countries. The preponderant and preferred term is 'government money' as though government is some far removed or detached entity, but whose presence and impact are overbearing and overwhelming nonetheless. This belief system has unfortunately led those appointed to positions of responsibility to view government as a milking cow to be exploited with impunity without accountability, limited only by the fear of the strong man president suspecting and identifying any challengers to his power. I touched on this in the preceding chapter by extensively quoting Professor George Ayittey, the Ghanaian renowned economist.

As long as those cronies and tribesmen and women steer clear of coveting the presidency itself, they can go on plundering the state coffers without regard to the consequences of their actions on the nation and wellbeing of its citizens. We covered this specific malaise extensively in the previous chapter. The only bright side has been Transparency International's annual report, which ranks countries on the corruption index. This ranking is starting to have some effect on these hitherto excesses.

Nevertheless, this has been only about ten years in the making and is not foolproof. To burnish their image, heads of state who feel embarrassed by these exposures are becoming conscious of this cancer and in response, some though few in number, are proceeding to prosecute a number of high ranking officials in their administrations, including seating government ministers. This patronage system is very widespread in most African countries.

With democracy never having been introduced and promoted by the administering foreign powers, most of those individuals who came to power at independence were more preoccupied with consolidating political power than worrying about economic development or democratic institutional development. Exacerbating these deficiencies is the fact that those visionary leaders and freedom fighters who fought and bled for independence were not those who were handed power upon its achievement.

The building of personal security apparatus via huge investments in the defense/security sector and the recruitment of loyalists to the strong men meant that very little resources were left available for economic development. From the outset, private entrepreneurial initiatives were frowned upon or scornfully discouraged. In many French speaking countries on the continent, these strong men presiding over weak national institutions only further exacerbated the cronyism and corruption by insisting on appointing everyone themselves—from managers of state corporations to regional or provincial governors right down to sub-district or local government levels.

With everyone looking forward to being appointed to alluring positions in both public and parastatal corporations, the job-creating small and medium size enterprises lagged far behind, further contributing to economic stagnation and underdevelopment. The veritable engine of development—small and medium sized enterprises—were left starved of national attention and adequate funding.

In many African countries, leaders have used their powers to punish or exclude the opposition and nonconformists while rewarding supporters and loyalists to the extent that the entrepreneurial spirit has been severely dampened. Some countries, particularly in French-speaking Africa, have bilateral military treaties, whereby France guarantees their "independence". But in practice, this guarantee is limited to maintaining the strong man in power, with little to no concern for defending the territorial integrity of concerned nations.

Ironically, it was French President, Charles de Gaulle, who famously stated that "When someone else is guaranteeing your independence, it means you no longer have sovereignty."[5] This was in opposition to Washington's dictates after World War II as the United States sought to shape the post-war world with such defense institutions as NATO. What France opposed then, she would pivot and impose on her ex-colonial 'independent' countries of Africa and elsewhere in the world, a glaring example of contradictions and hypocrisy of France's policies.

Exogenous Institutions

As earlier stated, African countries have been shaped by both indigenous and exogenous institutions over many decades. While internal structures and systems existed before the arrival of Europeans on the continent, the new institutions that were introduced by the newcomers have had lasting, but unfortunately, on balance, negative impacts on the continent, at least politically and economically speaking.

We saw above how the two principal European powers—Britain and France, employed different colonization methods in their respective colonies, leaving in their wake distinctive governmental systems that have thrived to this day, and upon which, political and economic decisions have been based, affecting the fortunes of countries and their populations differently.

Understanding Africa's situation becomes compounded by the development of supranational institutions such as the United Nations system, with its ancillary institutions like the World Bank, the International Monetary Fund and the International Finance Corporation.

African countries are further divided by numerous bilateral and multilateral treaties with their former colonial masters that range from English-speaking to French-speaking, and Spanish-speaking to Portuguese-speaking, and the linkages are very visible today. Language has never quite been divorced from culture as we see the wrangling and unnecessarily lengthy debates that occasionally characterize African Union summits when discussing the way forward for Africa.

Another relatively recent player on the continent has been the European Union (EU), which established "special" relations with all ex-European colonies. Some African scholars have wondered whether the EU was not formed as part of the design to maintain Africa under Europe's feet in cases where individual ex-powers were unable to do so.

While firm evidence does not exist to support this claim, the suspicion remains nonetheless. All these exogenous institutions have had and continue to have huge influence on the path that most of Africa should take politically and economically, sometimes with conflicting and overlapping recommendations.

Once signatory to the charters and internal rules of operations of these institutions, many an African country becomes bound by those rules, thus severely limiting independent sovereign actions. Even at the UN forum, hardly have Africans spoken with one voice on some very salient issues that affect the fortunes of the continent's peoples, leaving some observers aghast as some delegations take positions that mirror their former colonial masters, rather than pursuing policies that would benefit their collective countries.

Furthermore, and this has been proven, when the IMF makes loans to these African developing countries, the conditions are so overbearing that the indebted countries become further indebted, almost forever. This is because the terms are so one-sided and draconian that a huge chunk of the nation's foreign exchange revenue goes into servicing these loans to the detriment of social provisions and human capital investment. These international or supranational financial institutions literally force loans on African countries knowing fully well of their inability to repay. When these loans mature or become due, and the indebted countries find themselves unable to pay, these institutions rush to recommend privatization of state corporations and natural resources.

In many cases, the country's natural and national assets are used as collateral for loan approval and disbursement. As has been proven, their inability to repay or meet the conditionality leads to the indebted nations surrendering their national assets and resources to multinational corporations from developed, industrialized but mostly Western countries. These backhanded measures have been best described by John Perkins in his: *Confessions of an Economic Hitman*. This is just one of the many ways that billions of scarce financial resources flow out of Africa back to Europe in particular and the West in general.

Consequently, what was originally seen as a panacea agonizingly becomes an albatross as wealth continues an exodus from these countries to the richer, more advanced countries, further accentuating already unflattering poverty levels, perpetual dependency and gross underdevelopment.

With respect to Africa's relationships with these supranational and international organizations, not all is gloom and doom. Taken individually, the United Nations and its development organization—the United Nations Development Program, has played a positive role in promoting economic and institutional development and capacity building in Africa, especially when compared to the IMF and World Bank.

There is a recurring suspicion by African scholars and some national leaders that these two financial institutions are out to keep Africa economically depressed and dependent. They cite the Structural Adjustment Program (SAP) and other draconian protocols, which not only encourage mass discontent, but open their countries to multinational corporations by pushing for privatization and elimination of subsidies to state-owned development corporations.

This suspicion is so strong that some have dubbed the IMF the 'International Misery Fund' while others have called it the 'International Mafia Foundation.' These derisive characterizations come from having observed the political and social unrests, destabilization trends resulting from price increases that often accompany the implementation of these recommendations. When basic needs like electricity, water, food and transportation rise in costs to their populations, the majority of whom live on less than $2 a day, these imposed solutions are regarded as homicidal by the leaders and their advisers.

They may have a point because oftentimes, the local businesses lack the capital, technological know-how and experience to compete with foreign corporations that take over and raise prices, since they are strictly for-profit organizations. Whereas state-owned corporations and Public Private Partnerships have the social safety net component embedded in them. Evidence seems to have proven these suspicions legitimate. IMF/World Bank-prescribed solutions via its Structural Adjustment Program have led to social unrests and the toppling of governments in some developing countries in Africa and Latin America.

Proposed Solutions

For Africa to develop economically, each country's leadership, including civil society and all stakeholders, would have to undertake some fundamental reforms in all sectors of their societies:

1. First, no meaningful economic development would take place without relaxing control on both natural and human resources. By freeing up these resources, labor allocation would be more efficiently and productively employed. The current system of appointing unqualified individuals to manage parastatal business corporations based mostly on political and tribal considerations would have to be replaced by private sector employment of the best talents from a pool of qualified individuals.

2. There would have to be a conscientious effort on the part of national leaders to build strong institutions and legal frameworks that respect and protect private property rights. This would not become effective unless there is some real form of independent judiciary to litigate cases on their merits without political interference. The presidency in most African nations has too much sway over the judiciary, and this state of affairs is not reassuring

to investors and businesses whether these be local or foreign.

3. African governments would be better off putting into place tax incentives for business startups, tax moratoriums and exonerations from customs duties on certain imported equipment for business. Not only would these measures spur investment and reduce risks, but they would, in both short and long term, inevitably lead to increased employment, growth, expanded tax base and increased national GDP. Fortunately, though belatedly, quite a few handful of countries in Africa have undertaken reforms to entice investors. In practice though, the experience may be different.

Currently, educational institutions enjoy tax exemptions in many African countries, but governments would have to monitor these educational establishments to orient their curriculum towards Science, Technology, Engineering and Math (STEM) and the physical and natural sciences and management sciences with a view to creating future entrepreneurs, innovators and job creators.

4. Fourth, all of the above could be in place, but African nations would still seriously lag behind the rest of the world if key infrastructure is missing. Road infrastructure, reliable power or energy supply and reliable water resources are key and ongoing prerequisites for any meaningful national developmental take off. Oxfam and the World Bank estimate that in African countries, 2% to 4% or more of GDP is lost annually due to unreliable energy to power their economies. For detailed study on the economic costs to Africa's economy due to power shortages, power outages and energy deficiency as well as the average length of power outages, see Thomas Barnebeck and Carl Johan Darlgaard in "*Power Outages and Economic Growth in Africa*" (2013).[6] See also World Bank Enterprise Survey 2006-2010.[7]

Shane Kilfoil, CEO of energy giant, Eaton Africa, recommends fossil fuel would still be needed twenty to thirty years down the line to power African economies while still allowing for other forms of renewable energies like solar, wind, geothermal and hydro. Like him, I have no doubt that adequate energy would unlock the enormous economic potential of African economies and lift millions out of poverty. The alleviation of poverty on the continent is a priority. It is depressing to note that a United Nations 2013 study found that poverty on the continent rose from 290 million Africans in 1990 to 414 million in 2010. The underlying causes are many nonetheless with Illicit Financial Flows accounting for a huge proportion.

5. No workforce can contribute to any meaningful economic development if it is not educated and its members are unhealthy. So, naturally, other key areas that would need governments' focused attention are education and healthcare promotion. Africa's health sector is chronically underfunded, underdeveloped, underequipped and understaffed. Much needed attention and investment would be in order. A public-private partnership would go a long way in alleviating these sectorial problems. Literally billions of dollars are lost annually via brain drain of doctors to developed countries. While an average surgeon in the US earns some $220,000 annually, his counterpart in Africa earns between $14,000 to $30,000 per annum with some like in Kenya earning $6000 (WHO 2015).

6. Strict enforcement of these measures could begin to make a difference in the wellbeing of the citizenry. Enforcement is emphasized here as a key requirement for a holistic development because this is one domain that many African nations are notorious for. They specialize in crafting and making great laws and regulations for the books, but in practice, implementation is as far away as the north from the south poles. End users have been known to get frustrated while attempting to use the very well-written and attractive investment codes, for example, and some just give up and leave the countries concerned and move their businesses or endeavors elsewhere.

7. Another observed chronic deficiency in Africa is lack of maintenance and quality assurance. Once projects are built or put into place, ongoing maintenance and sustained quality assurance are seldom requirements. This fundamental lack of understanding of the value of maintenance and quality assurance in many African cultures has been known to cost nations and taxpayers billions

of dollars in rapid wear and tear and decay. Project life-spans are short-lived as a result of lack of maintenance and quality assurance.

8. Governments must take steps to protect nascent industries vis-a-vis foreign corporations, unless of course, those foreign-owned corporations decide to produce locally, thereby increasing not only national GDP, but fostering technology transfer to the local economy. This was one of the secrets that the much touted four small Asian dragons - namely Singapore, Hong Kong, Taiwan and South Korea used to be where they are today. Transformation of natural resources by both local and foreign corporations should be a national policy. Poverty reduction would be felt as employment figures soar. Africa cannot continue to remain the permanent source for raw materials while losing value added components of her natural resources.

9. One thing that is still critically lacking is seed money or venture capital for startups. Many young entrepreneurs have innovative business ideas, but the banking sector does not come through for them. Financial resources are in serious short supply as most well-capitalized banks are foreign-owned. The middle class is growing and in need of goods and services.

It is well-documented that Africa is the next frontier for wealth building and investment. Many young African college graduates are more prone to opening their own businesses than looking to government for jobs. And yet, local banks do not play their expected traditional roles of lending to finance projects. This is the case in Cameroon, specifically, despite the availability of profitable business ventures and a growing, vibrant middle class with needs to be met. Capitalization of existing financial institutions remains a problem to be seriously addressed.

In addition, it has been observed that many able investors don't invest in early startups, preferring to wait until a company is very successful before committing funds to its operations. As much as investments are always a private decision, I think that this 'wait and see success' attitude delays economic growth. This capitalization gap leaves a lot of young innovators starved of badly needed funds. It is widely understood that no business can grow without taking considerable, calculated risks, and the same applies for the economies of nations.

10. Enforce anti-graft laws, the absence of which results in billions of dollars sipping out of the economy. Some studies estimate that as much as $20 to 50 billion dollars per year leave the African continent to advanced, developed countries by politicians and other high government officials (OXFAM 2014).[8] Corruption kills a country's economy, and though this has not yet happened, it has certainly slowed economic growth and economic development thus exacerbating poverty. Embezzled funds that could have been used to capitalize local financial institutions and lend to local businesses for investment end up in foreign banks, serving same purposes in already developed countries. This and other practices led the UN to create in 2004 the High-Level Panel on Illicit Financial Flows headed by former South African president Thabo Mbeki (UN Statistics 2013).[9]

CHAPTER THREE

INTERNATIONAL TRADE AND GLOBALIZATION

The virtues of international trade cannot be overemphasized. Trade between nations positively contributes to national economic development. According to Europa magazine, published by the European Union, ten benefits are identified, especially as concerns developing countries. These are:

1. Trade can help boost development and reduce poverty by generating growth through increased commercial opportunities and investment, as well as broadening the productive base through private sector development. Between 2000 and 2008, GDP per capita rose from $326 to over $625 in less developed countries, and much of this income growth can be attributed to increased trade and foreign investment.

2. Trade facilitates export diversification by allowing developing countries to access new markets and new materials, which open new production possibilities. For example, India cut import duties from an average of 90% in 1991 to 30% in 1997. This gave Indian manufacturers access to a variety of intermediate and capital goods. Imports of intermediate goods increased by 227% over the same period. Two thirds of these intermediate goods were products India could not buy before 1991. As a result, industrial output grew by 50%, with new products accounting for 25% of the total.

3. Trade expands choice and lowers prices for consumers by broadening supply sources of goods and services and strengthening competition. Business-enabling reforms were undertaken and implemented in 36 Sub-Saharan African countries 2010/2011.

Of these, Mauritius ranks 23rd out of 183 countries in the World Bank's Ease of Doing Business report ahead of several EU member states.

Many African countries rank very far below despite having all these attractive investment codes on their books. Investors continue to face frustrating hurdles when it comes to practical application, with government officials expecting and demanding bribes. In some cases, these officials demand part ownership of the incoming businesses from investors without share capital input, trading their signatures for proposed company shares. This practice is more common in French-speaking Africa.

4. Trade plays a role in the improvement of quality, labor and environmental standards through increased competition and the exchange of best practices between trading partners, building capacity and product standards.

5. Trade strengthens ties between nations by bringing people together in peaceful and mutually beneficial exchanges, thereby contributing to peace and stability. This intuitive notion is confirmed by evidence. A study undertaken by the Center for Economic Policy Research on empirical data showed that the probability of disputes escalating into conflicts is lower for countries that trade more because of the opportunity cost associated with the loss of trade gains.

6. Trade enhances competitiveness by helping developing countries reduce the cost of inputs, acquire finance through investments, increase the added value of the products and move up the global value chain. Emerging economies like China, Brazil, India and South Africa are steadily catching up with developed countries, and it is thanks to increased trade. The per capita GDP increase of G20 developing countries stands at 115% for the decade of 2000 – 2010.

7. Trade contributes to cutting government spending by expanding supply sources of goods and services and strengthening competition for government procurement. This statement is only ideal in

countries where corruption is not widespread or rampant, and procurements are awarded on merits, not based on ethnic and nepotism factors. Government procurement usually makes up a considerable size of the market (often 10-15% of GDP) and the benefits for domestic and foreign stakeholders in terms of increased competition.

There is, however, a caveat here. It has also been observed that foreign companies from the former colonial master countries have an undue advantage over domestic competitors. They leverage political pressure and have greater capital outlays to bribe their way into government procurements than their domestic counterparts. Again, although an Africa wide phenomenon, this is very common in ex-French African countries. Newcomers like the Chinese have understood how to play the game and consequently, gain many government procurement contracts.

8. Trade creates employment opportunities by boosting economic sectors that create stable jobs and usually higher incomes, thus improving livelihoods. Manufacturing workers in open economies received pay rates that were 3 – 9 times greater than those in closed economies, depending on the region.

In Chile, and the same goes for such African countries like South Africa, Kenya and Botswana, a worker in a sector open to trade and investment gains an average $1,500 more per year than a worker in a relatively closed sector. This statement, again may be true for most countries, but not so in countries where political bosses influence employment patterns, and not the labor market.

9. Trade encourages innovation by facilitating exchange of know-how, best practices, technology and investment in research and development, including through foreign direct investment. Investment and trade have facilitated the deployment of information systems and telecommunications technology, with mobile cellular coverage reaching 86% of the population in 2008, including 69% of the African population.

10. Trade openness expands business opportunities for local

companies by opening up new markets, removing unnecessary barriers and making it easier for them to export. As afore-mentioned, business-enabling reforms were implemented in 36 Sub-Saharan African economies in 2010/2011. Of these, Mauritius ranks 23rd out of 183 countries in the World Bank's Ease of Doing Business Report ahead of several EU member states.[10]

Africa in International Trade: The Other Reality

Africa's share of international trade is a meager 3%. Unlike other world regions, intra-African trade is even more dismal, yet increased regional trade among African countries could exponentially boost prosperity in the continent. Intra-African trade is too low when compared to other world regions. Over the past decade, the share of intra-African trade in Africa's total trade was about 11% as compared to 21% for Latin America and the Caribbean, and 50% for the developing economies of Asia and 70% for Europe (UNCTAD, 2015).

While there is no denying that international trade has benefitted developing countries in the past, and may still be benefitting them today, we must also not lose sight of the other reality—that recent world economic slowdowns like the Great Recession of 2008/2009 wreaked unbearable havoc for developing economies, especially in Africa. That experience led to a rethinking of international trade and international finance as they impinge on developing economies. Equally noteworthy has been the slowdown in China's economic growth which is no longer the double-digit growth of the 90s and early part of the new millennium. As China's demand for purely raw natural resources has slowed as manufacturing gradually gives way to service and consumer sectors, these trends have affected Africa's economic fortunes.

Great care must be taken when discussing the advantages of international trade between developed and developing countries. Much of the literature on this subject lump together countries such as China, Brazil, India, and South Africa (BRICS), and sometimes, for reasons unknown to us, Russia. If not grouped as emerging markets or economies, they are often featured as developing. Yet, these categorizations mask the less developed countries of Africa, which for the most part, almost always find themselves at the shorter end of the world economic spectrum, largely due to them relying on commodities exports.

Few African countries' economies are export-based like the BRICS nations, so such comparisons distort the true picture of Africa's place in the world economy. Africa has not yet reached the stage that propelled the Southeast Asian nations to their economic miracles and placed some of them at same per capita GDP levels with European nations. Furthermore, despite so much talk of Africa being the next frontier of economic development and investment, I question the emphasis being placed on the rising consumer culture of the middle class.

Can consumption by this middle class, which requires services and trade in services, be enough to lift the continent out of poverty without adequate manufacturing or industrialization? Can expanded consumerism alone be a viable sustainable economic driver in Africa? The Asian economic miracles took place thanks to structural transformation that saw industrialization and export-driven economies. Is Africa's drive to growth based on trade in services and consumption of sophisticated goods and services be the answer?

Africa only boasts 3% of global commerce. It consumes only 3% of world energy, despite having 14% of the world's population. With the exception of South Africa, the rest of Africa has a chronic lack of necessary infrastructure and the industrial base to produce goods that are in demand both domestically and in developed countries. Durban is the only major container port on the continent among the top 100. Intra-African trade is dismal, although increasing. According to the World Bank, intra-African trade grew by 60% between 2010 and 2015, representing a rare ray of hope.

Despite recent progress made in inter-regional trade, the problem is still compounded by fifty-four border crossings, absent railway lines and poor roads—all resulting in high transport costs relative to other world regions. In spite of recent attempts at regional economic integration, the absence of transnational infrastructural assets like all-weather road networks, modern port facilities and railway lines, continue to hamper development across the continent.

Added to the above are suspicions on the part of oil-rich countries, which impose travel restrictions through visa requirements and high visa costs to discourage migration into their countries from resource-poor neighbors. The CEMAC/ECCAS zone of French-speaking countries is an example. There is greater movement of people, goods and services in the SADC and West African Economic zone—ECOWAS, than in the Central African economic zone—ECCAS.

These problems only further compound an already dire situation and the need for economic growth. The World Bank estimates that Africa would need $93 billion annually in critical infrastructure to close the development gap with the other regions of the world. One third of this amount would be required for maintenance alone. For Africa to transition from resource-based agricultural economy to a manufacturing industrial economy, it would require the constant and reliable supply of electricity, a critical need.

According to a 2014 report by the International Energy Agency, only 32% of Africans, or 1 out of 3, have access to electricity, leaving roughly more than 600 million men, women and children without power. Without electricity, hospitals cannot refrigerate medicines, children cannot do homework at night, and businesses cannot thrive.

Recognizing this fundamental need, US President, Barack Obama, launched an initiative called POWER AFRICA, with the goal of providing power to 60 million households by generating 30,000 megawatts of electricity. Congress is yet to vote to approve this measure and the outcome is uncertain as President Obama left office in January 2017 and the Trump Administration does not seem to prioritize that project with its insular policies.

Today, the average African pays more than 3.5 times the cost of per kilowatt of electricity than his American counterpart. The cost of electricity to run businesses takes up 10 – 15% of production costs, making African textiles uncompetitive on the world market. It is estimated that approximately 60 million generators are operating in Nigeria alone. This, for an oil exporting nation.

Globalization

Globalization, as I understand it, has its roots in the multinational corporations that grew out of the post-World War II era. The dominant power, the United States, seeing the need to reconstruct Europe economically, undertook the Marshall Plan, and by necessity, American businesses were those to produce the equipment, goods and services that were needed for reconstruction. The coming into existence of the Bretton Woods Institutions, the United Nations system and other international organizations in 1945 opened business opportunities for American companies to go global.

The markets were available, and the capital provided by the major banks was guaranteed by the US government. At one time, it was estimated that three out of every four Multinational Corporations (MNCs), or Transnational Corporations - (TNCs as some have called them), was American. It was natural for this dominance since Europe was in ruins and Japan was equally devastated.

This state of the world at that time allowed the US government, working hand in hand with American companies, to shape the current international political and economic systems in her image and interests, which still dominates the world till this day. Globalization can be seen as a normal growth or evolution of MNCs/TNCs with more potent tools such as the internet, which ensured the interconnectivity of the world we know today.

Transfer of technology took place from America to Europe and Japan, but not Africa, which being mostly made up of colonies then, was considered an appendage of Europe. Africa supplied the raw materials that fed the industrial rebuilding of Europe while America provided the capital and technology. This post-war set up and the colonization of Africa did not benefit the continent as it received no infused capital or transfer of technology.

This was the historical and structural base that has been responsible for Africa's economic woes to this day. The international system effectively placed Africa at huge disadvantages administratively, politically and economically. Democracy was never encouraged, free press was a far-off idea only good for Europe and America, and private sector initiatives were shunned for Africa, as was education. Roads were constructed only to ferry raw materials from the hinterlands to the seaports on the coast for evacuation to Europe. Railway lines were built for a similar purpose—to transport raw materials to the coastal towns for onward shipment to Europe.

Economic and Wealth Disparities

This is one issue that has spurred passionate debates among conflicting schools of thought from many scholars and practitioners of development. We shall examine some key components of this issue, highlighting pros and cons as are related to the prescriptions of the IMF and World Bank on the economies of African nations.

First, to put things in perspective, I shall present some startling statistics to help us better appreciate the magnitude of this problem, which by a growing number of accounts, threatens national cohesion in both developed and developing countries. According to Oxfam and Forbes, 1% of the world's richest will own 50% of the planet's wealth while the poorest 80% owned 5.5% in 2016. The causes of these disparities are many, and in the previous chapter, we covered the endogenous causes. Furthermore, as per OXFAM and theRules. org, MNCs, the main drivers of these widening gap between the few super wealthy and the growing poor of the world can be seen in the following. The wealthiest 62 percent of people on this planet own as much wealth as the bottom half of humanity or some 3.6 billion people. The top 1 percent in 2016 owned more wealth than the bottom 99 percent who live in poverty, unemployment with little to no education, healthcare, housing and drinkable water. The gap keeps widening in developed as well as developing countries.

In the United States, the champion of free trade in the past but now pushing for fair trade, income and wealth disparities are giving rise to anti-immigrant xenophobic right-wing politicians. In the last fifteen years, some 60,000 manufacturing factories have closed and left for low wage countries as per Senator Bernie Sanders, the democratic presidential candidate. Some 4.8 million well paid manufacturing jobs are gone permanently due to corporate outsourcing. Despite an increase in productivity, the average male American worker earns $726 less per year in 2016 than he did in 1973 (Senator Sanders). while the average female American worker earns $1154 in 2016 than she earned in 2007 after adjusting for inflation. Some 47 million Americans live in poverty with 28 million without health insurance. Still in the US, the top one tenth of 1 percent now owns more wealth than the bottom 90 percent of citizens while 58 percent of new income is going to the top 1%.

These are today's fact sheets on the American economy and the question is should African countries continue the Western economic model? This economic model was set up by the economic elite for the benefit of the economic elite and prescribed through the Bretton Woods institutions and the MNCs. With so much disparities and growing despondency across the globe, it is almost conclusive the Washington Consensus has failed and continue failing hundreds of millions of humanity.

The downside of unbridled free enterprise and privatization of state-owned corporations like railways, ports, electricity, gas and water utilities is not only bad for African economies, but bad for national cohesiveness. Yet, these are measures the IMF and World Bank prescribe for African leaders.

Evidence increasingly shows that the corporations from the developed world easily take over domestic businesses once the loans advanced to these developing countries cannot be repaid since the loans are collateralized against commodities and other national assets, notably public utilities.

In the developed economies where an annual GDP growth of 3% is considered good enough, the income disparities are becoming wider with each passing year. This phenomenon has been identified as the primary and principal cause of economic downturn in these advanced countries.

The reason is simple: as the middle class disappears steadily and the lower class keeps burgeoning, there will inevitably come a time when the lower, poorer class would have no finances left to afford the goods and services available in the economy.

We know that demand spurs production or aggregate output, hence supply. With most of their money having been sucked up by the richest 1%, the drop in demand would mean continuous contraction of the economy with attendant results of lay- offs, company closures, outsourcing, social tensions and eventually, national economic collapse. This outcome would come about as the tax base for government programs would dry up, further running up the national debt and deficit. These are prescriptions for disaster, and the developing countries would be ill-advised to accept these doomed-to-fail recommendations.

The only conclusion one can take away from what is happening currently and has been the case for more than two decades now, is that the so-called trickle-down economic development theory has failed as a model in its present form. Developing countries of Africa who face both structural, historical and modern-day onslaughts from various angles would be better off reexamining these recommendations.

The nascent industries must be protected from mega MNCs, lest they get wiped out and/or end up with raw deals like in the case of Guinea, where ALCOA has been exploiting the country's bauxite for more than five decades while contributing very little to its treasury. ALCOA is an American mining company owned by CBG, Inc. Since 1960, it has been mining bauxite from Guinea, a country where 55% of the population live below the poverty level of less than $2.00 per day, and where 1 in 5 people lack access to electricity. That country, according the World Bank and UN ranking, is the 10th poorest country on earth.

Since 1960, over $400 billion has been sucked out of the country from mining this mineral alone, and as is commonly the case, ALCOA has never honored the terms of agreement that it made with the Government of Guinea for a fair share of the revenue from this product, and neither has it honored the transportation component entered into with that country's national shipping line for a fixed percentage of the shipment. This example further illustrates the unchecked power wielded by these foreign multinational corporations and the corresponding weakness of host African countries.

Another MNC, French energy giant AREVA has been exploiting uranium in Niger for six plus decades without paying anything significant into that country's treasury. Were it not for the UNCTAD that has recently taken up the complaints of these poor exploited African countries to address this tax avoidance activities by MNCs, Niger's vital mineral used for nuclear power production would continue being exploited without contributing to the country's economy. Paying its fair share of due taxes would provide badly needed revenue that could be used for poverty reduction measures and provide social and human services to improve livelihoods of the Nigerien people. According to Professor Mark Curtis, former Research Fellow at the Royal Institute of International Affairs (Chatham House) in a study titled "*Britain's New African Empire*", companies listed on the London Stock Exchange control over $1 trillion worth of Africa's resources in just five commodities- oil, gold, diamonds, coal and platinum. According to a research he carried out for the NGO named **War on Want**, which has just been published revealed that 101 companies, most of them British, control $305 billion worth of platinum, $276 billion worth of oil, and $216 billion worth of coal at current market prices. From Tanzania's gold to Zambia's copper to South Africa's platinum and gold and diamonds, London listed companies control and own mines in 37 African countries with concessions covering a staggering 1,03 million square kilometers on the continent. This is over four times the size of the UK and nearly one-twentieth of Sub-Sahara Africa's total land area. While these non-African owned African mines are in themselves revolting, this situation is further exacerbated by the non-payment of a fair share of taxes, royalties and other emoluments to the African governments for national development purposes. The same study estimates that Africa loses more than $46 billion annually in outgoing profits via tax dodging and tax havens, mostly in the British Virgin Islands. Africa which is rich in natural resources, but poor in socioeconomic wellbeing is further impoverished by the Western powers, principally, US, UK and France.

Moreover, and sadly so, these corporations are loyal to no one country, but to their shareholders, even though their governments would not hesitate to intervene militarily to "protect" their so-called "national interests"—a term that they broadly define and apply unilaterally. Here again lies the contradictions. MNCs are not really loyal to the citizens or national wellbeing of the countries they operate out of, nor are they loyal to the countries they operate in.

Nonetheless, they would readily call upon their willing and ready home office governments to intervene on their behalf, diplomatically, politically and if all else fails, militarily, to maintain their privileged positions of exploitation of poorer countries' economies. By some estimates, within the past thirty years, Africa has lost more than 1 trillion dollars to the West (OXFAM).[11]

How Africa Loses Funds through International Trade

According to the Guardian News Magazine and the United Nations Economic Commission for Africa (UNECA), large multinational corporations have taken more than $900 billion between 1970 and 2008 from the continent through fraudulent tax arrangements. From Africa alone, approximately $50 billion is lost every year through illicit financial outflows as governments and MNCs engage in fraudulent schemes to avoid taxes, and mispricing of goods through subsidiaries. According to the same report, $200.17 billion was illicitly taken out of Nigeria within the same period, while

Egypt lost $105.2 billion and South Africa more than $81.8 billion.

Added to the above figures, poor countries lose $600 billion each year on debt servicing or interest payments on loans. Through unfair trade rules imposed by the West multilaterally, poorer countries lose another $500 billion each year (University of Massachusetts Dept. of Economics).[12] The majority of these illicit transfers originate from West Africa, accounting for about 38% of the $50 billion annual outflow. Commodity products, which form the bulk of the developing world's export, have their prices set in Western capitals. For example, coffee and cocoa prices are set in London while other prices are set in New York.

A very disturbing trend in international trade as carried out by mostly Western MNCs is the potential loss of national sovereignty whereas, these MNCs are seeking to weaken governments and rewrite laws that would shield them from class action suits for non-compliance. They are pushing for dismantling of all regulations by governments in the countries they operate businesses to ensure profits never reduce. By trying to influence the WTO, they hope to control countries and governments under the guise of "Free Trade" and eliminate labor unions and weaken their power to demand better working conditions and other worker benefits such as medical care and reasonable pension packages. By going through the WTO, these could become binding on member countries- a frightening scenario for national sovereignty and rights over their natural resources. These measures must be collectively resisted. In effect, they want to be able to sue governments if their laws make them lose profits, refuse paying taxes or compensation for damages to the local water supply, land and environmental pollution.

The problem faced by African commodity exporting countries is that since they were maneuvered into agreeing to deregulation and elimination of price stabilization funds to move into the derivative pricing structure, they are at the mercy of the developed countries.

Derivative markets simply mean that a developing country agrees to future prices of their commodities in advance, which could be years to a decade. These arrangements do not preclude spot market exchanges for sellers and buyers. It is akin to mortgaging the future by fixing set prices in the future regardless of how demand might be in that future. If demand increases, prices are not affected and the producer nations cannot reap the benefits of rising demand, hence greater revenue that would have accrued therefrom.

On the flip side, however, a depressed market should benefit the producer nations. But history has shown that in very rare cases or scenarios does demand fall or do prices drop drastically although it could happen like with oil glut. The recent drop in oil prices appears to be artificially triggered for political objectives by the biggest oil producers and has little or nothing to do with normal demand and supply. Commodity-exporting countries are impacted by the price volatility in the commodities markets of London, New York and Chicago.

The amplitude of price changes can be quick, delivering unexpected shocks to the economies of producer countries, and making budgetary and development planning an onerous task for governments. However, according to data from the United Nations Conference on Trade and Development (UNCTAD), commodity-exporting African countries have had a windfall for the last decade from rising prices of their commodities. Oil has been the exception as we know, but that cycle of high commodity prices has ended as demand slows down in China.

Since under IMF and World Bank recommendations, which saw massive deregulation of the commodities institutions, the elimination of Price Stabilization Institutions in developing countries in favor of open market, spot markets, derivatives and futures markets, the bag has had mixed results. As bankers, traders and other financial instruments were brought in to play larger roles in these markets, they can influence price structures to gain leverage.

The Greatest Threat to Peasant Land Holdings

A more dangerous outcome of these IMF recommended measures is the risks that investors are now looking at Africa's arable lands, which comprise 60% of world total, to cultivate farmlands using machinery to increase production for export. The implications are ominous as these large corporations could displace local peasant farmers and turn them into landless tenants. The latter could lose century old ownership of their lands that have sustained their families for centuries. It happened in Latin America, so African governments must take note and take measures to avoid what happened to the landowners of South America in the name of modernized agriculture.

Cash crops take precedence over food crops that ensure food security, and if, suddenly, the villagers find themselves without their primary source of living—their family farms—they risk being turned into grocery shoppers with the kind of low per capita income of less than $2 a day that they have, and have had, for decades. When hedge fund managers begin to enter the commodities futures market like they have in the stock market for decades, there becomes a cause for alarm.

The world economy has not fully recovered from the derivatives triggered stock market crash—the Great Recession that hit the world in 2008/2009 and was particularly financially hard on several African economies. Additionally, the macroeconomic factors cannot be ignored as commodity markets become more financialized. Speculation is increasingly entering the commodity markets, and this is where the risks lie. Prediction becomes less and less possible as banks and hedge fund managers become the central players. These sophisticated financial instruments and actors have been too difficult for cooperatives, governments and commodity traders to understand, much less compete.

Whether we look at cotton in Burkina Faso, coffee in Ethiopia, or coffee and cotton in Mozambique, all these countries often bear the brunt of international price fluctuations as traders and managers interact in the commodity markets. Intra-seasonal factors do also cause price volatility, regardless of liberalized markets like Tanzania, or producer-protected national stabilization systems as in Mozambique and Burkina Faso. As a matter of fact, most producer countries often suffer from price fluctuations, and this should be expected to continue as banks, investors and traders carry out trading activities through futures and derivatives markets.

Recommendations

After holistically examining the problems faced by commodity exporting countries, I make the following recommendations:

1. The first action by the governments of developing countries in Africa should be to strive to reduce dependency on the export of raw materials and instead push for transformation as well as

manufacturing value addition.

2. They should enter into negotiations to gain better terms of trade between their countries and the developed countries, so as to arrive at mutually beneficial and fair-trade rules.

3. They should diversify their revenue sources by budgetary outlays that emphasize local manufacturing and services. Domestic demand is rising as the middle class grows.

4. Nationals should be trained to better understand the new landscape that has seen new actors like banks, hedge fund managers, insurance schemes and derivatives. This would strengthen the developing countries' bargaining position vis-a-vis these new sophisticated actors who have come onboard.

5. They should also seek assistance from the developed world in financing infrastructure such as farm-to-market, farm-to-manufacturing plants, road and railway lines, port facilities and telecommunications technology. Through telecommunications, producers can be informed in a timely manner on market conditions, climatic conditions and soil fertility. The need to seek assistance should not mean long-term foreign aid dependent development that could compromise national sovereignty. Interdependence should not mean surrender of national sovereignty.

Foreign Aid

Proponents of foreign aid are always quick to point to data that shows foreign direct official aid and Foreign Direct Investments from the rich, advanced countries to developing countries. What is almost always missing is data on the amount of funds that flow from developing countries to these rich, advanced economies. We shall examine these reverse flows to have a better and more complete picture.

We just saw how much funds are leaving the poor countries to finance the richer countries through fraudulent financial and tax schemes between MNCs and governments. Rich countries give a total of $130 billion annually to developing countries as foreign aid, but that is nothing when compared to the over $1.2 trillion dollars taken out each year by these MNCs from Africa, in particular, and developing countries in general, to developed economies (TheRules. org, 2015).[13]

One factor that we must not ignore is the support the West lends to corrupt African leaders, thereby propping them up to continue exploitation of these poor countries. Instead of working to better the wellbeing of their fellow citizens, these self-serving leaders work to maintain the interests of their foreign backers and their interests. Africa's dream of becoming a united, strong global player in the world would be seriously set back unless a new crop of visionary, selfless leaders take over the reins of power and decision making. We do not expect the West to sit idly without sabotaging the continent's drive toward a continental government with a single currency and parliament. They have their job cutout for them by the multiplicity of languages and colonial legacies. These apparent weaknesses notwithstanding, we still believe a determined crop of new, courageous and savvy leaders would be able to present a united front as they engage the rest of the world, finding and forging new friends and alliances without foregoing old ones. For, at the end of the day, a strong united developed and democratic Africa would be good for the global community.

The Risks to Governments

Africa is arguably the most resource endowed continent on the planet. Her natural resources have been exploited by European countries for well over a century, and yet, the motherland still has plenty of what the world economy needs. This blessing may have turned out to be a curse at the same time, since foreign countries, through their multinationals and neighbors of certain countries such as the Democratic Republic of Congo, intervene to claim a piece of her wealth. This country is so rich that its coveted resources have placed the country in perpetual civil war, encouraged by competing outside powers for over a decade, and resulting in the loss of millions of lives.

The beleaguered country has been described as the richest piece of real estate on the planet. It has oil, manganese, coltan, cobalt, gold, diamonds and more in large quantities. It has equally been described by many observers in this telling manner, "The Greatest Curse of the DRC is its Wealth." The DRC contains 64% of world total reserves of a very rare but important black mineral, without which the world would have no cell phones. It is used in tablets, airplane turbine fans, computers and other electronic equipment. Its importance is found in its high resistance to corrosion. Coltan or Columbite Tantalite. As the global automobile industry increasingly switch from petroleum to electric battery powered vehicle engines, the DRC which has two thirds of the world's cobalt - over 60%, risks becoming embroiled in more conflicts. This is already happening as that country's government seeks to double the price of this precious metal which the Western automobile makers such as Tesla, Volkswagen, General Motors, Ford and Toyota Motor Company need, but aren't willing to pay a fair price that could uplift the lives of the Congolese people. Remarkably, the Catholic church in that country has joined the chorus asking Joseph Kabila to step down since his term expired. Question is what about long serving dictators in many African countries who have been in power for three or more decades and changed their countries constitutions to eliminate term limits? Once more, we see hypocrisy and attempts to get Africa's resources for free.

Despite all these mineral resources, the DRC ranks among some of the planet's poorest countries. With a population of over 77 million (2015), its GDP stands only at $35 billion with majority population living on less than $200 a day. Despite registering a 6.9 % growth rate in 2015, the country is still experiencing grinding poverty among competing interests within Africa and outside the continent.

According to the UN, in the last fifteen years, there have been more than five million deaths, 300,000 women raped and millions more displaced in the DRC due to conflicts, as countries and companies alike vied for control of the African nation's rare minerals (UN Stat, 2003). Sadly though, the country ranks last in the UN's Human Development Index. Thus, goes the paradox.

Some statistics should shed light on some of these resources. Africa is home to 40% of the world's gold, 60% of cobalt, 90% of platinum and 60% of the world's arable land. With so much at play, conflicts are inevitable, as everyone would want a piece of it, disregarding whether or not they were entitled to them as we saw in the DRC example above. This is where great risks are encountered by the national leaders of those resource-rich African countries.

The rising middle class, with its political and economic power, is already forcing and demanding changes in the distribution of resources. Most countries have about 70 or 80% of their population in agriculture. Of the unemployed, the youth make up 60% and more in some countries. This is particularly troubling for national leaders who must find ways of absorbing these numbers into the workforce. About 72% of them live on less than $2.00 a day.

While their desires for better lives increase exponentially, their means grow arithmetically at best, putting them on a collision course with hopelessness. Their skills and education are inadequate or falling short of company expectations, and the invisible hand of the market is holding them down.

This is another example where trickle-down economics has failed millions of able-bodied men and women. Without a job, they cannot afford housing. Without housing, they cannot get married, and without marriage, they are stuck in a suspended state of late adolescence and unmet ambitions. Cameroonians and dozens of young Africans lost an entire decade of the 80s due to joblessness.

Bursting with energy, teeming with ambition, armed with modern tools of information in their palms, these armies of unemployed pose significant risks to policy makers all across Africa. Rampant unemployment of the young could lead many to seek glory and self-worth in extremism, notably, the Islamist terrorist group, Boko Haram, which has already killed up to 12,000 innocent civilians in Nigeria and Cameroon while displacing millions more.

The President of Cameroon is sitting on a tinderbox in a country where the average age of the population is 19. Governments don't seem prepared to provide jobs for 10 – 12 million young people who enter the labor market each year with less than 5% having university degrees to their names. In Cameroon and some other African countries, national leaders have found what I term a palliative solution to rampant unemployment by encouraging the young and mostly non-university segment of their populations to engage in motor bike transportation in urban and rural areas. This sector has absorbed hundreds of thousands, if not millions of young men into self-employment. But this development has come with its own costs. The sheer numbers of these motor taxis that go by different names in different African countries are causing annoying traffic nightmares to drivers and other urban dwellers. They have become a real nuisance in the large urban areas to the consternation of many. Second, labor shortages are acute in the agricultural sector as three in four unemployed uneducated youth now dream of owning and operating a motor bike taxi. As income of households are low, and parents cannot afford tuition in secondary and university education, some parents are opting to pay for a motor taxi rather than send their children to secondary and university education. The ramifications for a future economy are causes for concern as the quality of future workforce would be lower in an increasingly sophisticated and competitive world economy. Third, these young men of today shall become the old men of tomorrow and how sustainable would this trade be as they grow old with slacking reflexes and no retirement plans or funds saved up? These are important questions that must be addressed, and it is precisely for these three reasons that I referred to this motor bike taxi operations encouraged by governments as palliative.

While most African countries made impressive gains in the primary educational level between 2000 and 2012 toward the Millennium Development Goals set by the United Nations, the same cannot be said of secondary and higher education. In addition, these gains were offset by population increases. According to UNESCO, 35% more children needed teachers, books, and safe learning environments in 2012 than they did in 2000.[14]

Unfortunately, the desire to learn is often crushed by inefficiently allocated resources, with corruption and revolving door practices swallowing up a significant percentage of budgetary outlays in the public school systems. Public school classrooms have 70 – 80 pupils per class, rendering it impossible for teachers to give individualized attention to pupils. If these armies of young job-seekers are not well managed, they could turn out to be an explosive force, which once unleashed, would be unable to contain.

It is widely known that Octogenarians rule many African countries, a trend that may well signify Africa's most tragic flaw. The old hang on to power too long and thereby, prolong the day the next generations would take over the reins of leadership. It has been estimated that most African presidents are fifty years older than the average age of their fellow citizens (Hruby, 2015).[15]

In their article, 'The Next Africa: An Emerging Continent becomes a Global Powerhouse,' Jack Bright and Aubrey Hruby state, "Humanity's past is in Africa and its future is increasingly in Africa. By 2050, Africa is projected to have 1 billion people in the workforce" (Bright & Hruby, 2015).[16]

One cannot honestly discuss the problem of income disparities without addressing the notion of inequality of opportunities. That's where focus should be and we will examine this issue in depth.

Inequality of Income and Opportunities

Inequality of opportunities is attributed to the differences in circumstances beyond one's control such as gender, tribe, location at birth, or language. Inequality of outcomes arises from a combination of differences in opportunities and individual talent and efforts. One cannot equally separate effort from intergenerational context. Stated differently, parental income plays an important role in determining fortunes and opportunities that their children would or would not have.

Parents with higher incomes can afford better schools for their children, thus increasing their chances/opportunities to earn better income after graduation than children whose parents cannot afford such education (IMF, 2015).[17] There is a correlation between higher disposable income and higher economic growth. Also, Rawls (1971)[18] has argued that the distribution of opportunities and outcomes are equally important and informative to understand the nature and extent of inequality around the world.

All these notwithstanding, some degree of inequality must exist in any society to stimulate incentives such as hard work, smart work, creativity, competition, investment savings, etc. to move ahead in life. As long as inequality is not extreme or deliberately institutionalized by the political elite based on color, race, ethnicity, gender, religion or language, some modicum of inequality is welcome and plays a positive role in stimulating innovations by entrepreneurial individuals to create job opportunities while adding to GDP and economic growth.

However, when inequality is manufactured via a deliberate policy by government, labor resources and natural resources are misallocated, leading to negative economic consequences for that country.

When a few powerful but greedy group of men manipulate and intimidate the political elite to disproportionately amass wealth for themselves and their immediate families, inequality becomes not only a political and socioeconomic problem, but a psychological one as well. Such circumstances would create injustices and would also be considered denial of basic human rights.

No one has placed this problem better than Rev Kyrsoibor Pyrtuh (2016)[19] , writing for theRules.org, when he states, "Inequality becomes a struggle for truth and justice. There is nothing judgmental about truth and justice as rather, these two important pillars of society are transformative, redemptive and creative in character."

Where there is a state of significant economic inequality in any society, citizens lose confidence in national institutions, social cohesion is weakened, national unity is threatened, progress is compromised, and the country slides into dictatorship with dire consequences for the nation such as civil strife and conflicts.

This state of affairs could open up the country to enemies from outside via disgruntled citizens and to conflicts whose resolution becomes increasingly difficult. Furthermore, extreme inequality kills growth drivers such as education, health, incentives to invest or save, and innovations, resulting in poor and slower labor productivity and mobility (Stiglitz, 2012)[20] .

Inequality in health outcomes is very widespread in African countries, and access to the limited facilities leaves a large percentage of the population without adequate healthcare. Africa is further beset by the brain drain of trained doctors that leave Africa for greener pastures - mainly, the USA. The World Health Organization estimates that in most African countries, there is 0.15 doctors to a 100,000 population. Some countries have even lower; .50 doctors to each 100,000 people. What is troubling is the practice of high government officials who evacuate themselves and family members to get quality treatment in developed countries instead of encouraging growth and improvements in domestic healthcare. There needs to be priority investment in the health sector and incentives must be put into place to attract both African trained doctors and Western or European trained specialists. It is estimated that this brain drain is costing Africa more than $4 billion dollars annually. This problem's resolution is handicapped by the tendency of politicians to invest in their security and longevity in power by procurement of expensive state of the art security equipment and apparatus and paying security personnel disproportionally much higher than professionals such as doctors and engineers. In some countries, each general is dotted with a budget and no accountability exist as to how the funds are spent. No reporting system exist.

Moreover, infant mortality is twice as high in developing countries as in developed ones. Roughly 60% of the poorest youth population (aged 20 – 24) in Sub-Saharan Africa have fewer than five years of schooling, compared to 15% in developed countries. The importance of education cannot be overemphasized as it goes without saying that the more educated citizens have a better chance to adapt to technological developments than their less educated counterparts.

CHAPTER FOUR

GOVERNANCE

Political Reforms

Africa is so huge, its national systems of government so diverse, and its foreign interests so pervasive that no one set of possible solutions would suffice to tackle the problems currently facing the 55 nations that make up the continent. African leaders would have to undertake far reaching reforms of their countries' political systems, thereby allowing for greater liberal economic and political systems that would attract greater participation in the political process. A deliberate move would be required to assemble all major stakeholders within each country to ensure that strong institutions are in place, rather than strong men who eternalize power.

The current overconcentration of power and over centralization of administration would have to give way to semi-autonomy for the provinces and regions, allowing the locals to elect their governors. If governors are elected, rather than appointed by the heads of state, they would become more responsible and accountable to their constituents, not to the president in some far away capital city. The current practice of the presidents appointing government officials—from governors all the way down to the lowest city council government delegates—as is the case in Cameroon, only encourages misplaced loyalty, corruption, impunity and abuse of power.

Just as the installed presidents following independence in 1960 looked up to and were dependent on Paris for staying power and decision-making guidelines, so too are today's appointed governors and administrators dependent on and answerable only to the heads of state. This has not worked well for both economic and social development, nor has it contributed to genuine national unity, national integration or the much-cherished patriotism. In its place have been tribalism, cronyism, nepotism and provincialism, manifesting themselves in inefficient allocation of national and labor resources.

When a large percentage of a country's population feel left out and have no incentives to identify with a national territory, or have no confidence in national institutions, the results are resignation, frustration, and potential for irredentism. Many African strongmen leaders think they can decree patriotism or national unity. It would never happen.

On the contrary, in so doing, they are sowing the seeds of political instability, and with political instability, domestic and foreign investors get chased away. The reason is simple. No one, local or foreign, would want to invest in or settle to do business in any country where the security environment is uncertain.

The constitutions of many African countries need to be revised and term limits placed on political leaders despite the trend to the contrary as seen recently. The military should be trained to protect the national territory and citizens, not one man - the commander-in-chief. A complete shift in mentality would be needed to begin to achieve this particularly vital goal.

Furthermore, enforceable anti-corruption laws would be required by a parliament that is not under the personal control of the president. Also, a truly independent judiciary with powers to impeach and jail presidents or their cabinet ministers and other high-level parastatal members would have to be instituted. A June 2016 law in Cameroon that was tabled by government to give immunity to ministers - members of government from prosecution is an anachronism pure and simple. This is essentially a green light that they can embezzle without fear of being imprisoned. It is clearly a setback in fighting corruption that is already so widespread. Fortunately, and thanks to the protest march by the English-speaking lawyers in the city of Bamenda, the president rejected the bill passed by both houses of Parliament that had ostensibly given immunity to government ministers. This is a victory for the people and the president who would have been hoodwinked into signing a bad piece of legislation.

A partially free press or a mixed public-private press would be essential to keep both elected and appointed officials on the right track.

Why a *partially* free press? Well, the truth is, a completely free press may not exist anywhere in the world. It has been noted that the mainstream media in the US is corporate-owned and their editorial policies are being increasingly dictated by their corporate owners. This trend is bad for true democracy. This tendency in the US is worrisome as the super-rich 1% continue to squeeze out the lower 99%, buying up and taking ownership over the media and consolidating more financial power, leading some voices to an outcry that soon democracy, as was conceived and intended, would no longer work.

Economic Reforms

African countries should resist the recommendations of the IMF and World Bank with respect to total privatization of state enterprises. Often, the countries' commodities and other natural resources are taken over for free when the indebted nations cannot pay back loans. Most spend decades only servicing those loans, and this stunts economic development, with potential for political instability and social unrests.

Whenever a country is judged to be unstable politically, investors withhold decisions, and FDI dries up, further depressing the economy. Trade terms should be negotiated with fairness to all parties, and African countries must insist on the development of value added transformative industrial activities. The private sector should be encouraged, but taxation tools could be used to provide guidelines to avoid extreme income inequalities.

Moreover, equality of opportunities should be codified, and talents and innovative entrepreneurs supported by government funding. Economic opportunities would bring forth these talents in every sector, ranging from healthcare to education to technological innovations. Labor resources would be more efficiently allocated or distributed, culminating in expanded economic growth and development as the tax base becomes expanded.

For French speaking Africa, a concerted effort would have to be made for each country to print its own national currency, just as Nigeria, Ghana, and Botswana and Kenya have done, until there comes into existence a pan-African united, single currency. As long as they are lumped into the French-linked francs that does no longer exists and their reserves kept in the French government treasury abroad, economic development shall continue to be an elusive goal for these African nations.

Remittances

Remittances by the African diaspora have proven to be an important source of financing for many economies on the home continent. Family members living abroad send to their families substantial sums that meet needs from education, healthcare, housing and small business operations. These remittances contribute to better wellbeing.

According to BBC's Mark Doyle, Africans' remittances outweigh Western Aid. Africans send more money to Africa than Official Development Assistance (ODA). In 2010, the African diaspora remitted a total of $51.86 billion to the continent. In the same year, the World Bank sent $43 billion to Africa. According to data retrieved from Prof Adams Bodomo of Hong Kong University, 75% of remittances to Africa are sent by informal channels.[21] This tells us that the actual amount may, in fact, be greater.

Globally, ODA accounts for $130 billion to developing countries each year, which pales when compared to Diaspora remittances of $350 billion. This figure includes China, India and Brazil, in addition to Sub-Saharan Africa. Generally, Africans try to avoid the high transmission fees that banks charge, which hover around 12% of total funds. To further understand what is happening with these issues of financial outflows and inflows, it is important to look at these data from the African Development Bank, the OECD and UNDP. According to these three institutions, Foreign Direct Investment to Africa in 2015 amounted to $55.26 billion while remittances by the African diaspora came to $64.6 billion and Official Development Assistance was $54.9 billion.

Western Union and MoneyGram are the most widely used channels for foreign remittances, given their relatively lower fees. Funds from the Diaspora go a long way in alleviating poverty, since these funds go directly to end users in both urban and rural areas. This is especially true in rural areas, where in most cases, the formal banking infrastructure and government outlays do not reach or are less impactful.

Remittances are not limited to sending funds to relatives at home for personal use, although the bulk of these remittances go to relatives for tuition, livelihoods, health care, education and family housing construction and remodeling. Dr. Ben Page, of the Royal Geographic Society and Professor of Human Geography at University College London, asserts other components of Diaspora contribution to local level economic development. As he asserts from having conducted research in Cameroon for two decades, interacting with villagers and urbanites, some in the Diaspora have created what he calls Home Town Associations or HTAs.[22]

HTAs are organizations grouping Diaspora elements from the same villages, towns or regions, where members come together periodically - usually annually, to identify projects, contribute and raise funds to channel back to their villages of origin. Among such projects are financing the construction of amenities and facilities ranging from morgues, primary and secondary school classrooms to dispensaries and supply of medical equipment such as beds, computers and training.

Some of these organizations are well-structured and managed by elected members who are accountable to their members, often undergoing spot audits to ensure accountability and efficient management of funds so raised or contributed. Some well-developed Diaspora HTAs have significant impact on the home communities they serve back in their villages of origin, such as the Bali Development and Cultural Association founded in the USA which goes by the acronym BCA-USA with branches in many European countries.

This organization is one of the most often cited for commendable works and has been existing for almost three decades. The BCA-USA has built schools, improved their fon's palace, and have even taken up the payment of teachers' salaries in some schools. They have also built Technical Training Centers and continue to train young people of both genders in skill sets such as carpentry, metallurgy and welding, building design and construction, cosmetology, tailoring and embroidery, and computer learning, just to cite a few areas sponsored by this particular HTA.

According to Samba and Le Masson (2005),[23] the 20,000 Cameroonians in the US have an annual purchasing power of $10 billion). With this kind of purchasing power, committed and caring Diaspora members can afford to aid the development effort in their country of origin and improve the livelihoods of loved ones.

Kingsley Awang Ollong (2013),[24] author of 'The Cameroonian Diaspora: Its Role in Local Development,' further states, "The Diaspora's contribution is equally found in innovative ideas, intellectual capacities and skills and creative business practices from the West to Cameroon. According to this same source, the 57,000 Cameroonians living within the European Union remitted an official total of $2.0003 million in 2006 to Cameroon. When the informal transfer channels are included, this figure is bound to be higher.

Another informal channel used by Africans to transfer funds to their countries of origin by the Diaspora in the US and the EU is swapping. Using this method, a financially viable relative or person back in Africa with children in universities in the US and EU hands over the funds agreed upon to the organizations or relatives while the Diaspora deposits the corresponding amount to their student/children in their country of residence. The sometimes-exorbitant transfer fees are thus avoided, but the transaction is complete. Naturally, this practice requires mutual trust by both parties, and there have been no scandals or litigation arising from this informal fund transfer thus far.

As can be seen, these remittances have proven to be important, reliable lifelines and sources of income to extended family members, organizations and local communities from the Diaspora. Lastly, some HTAs have been known to provide seed money for small businesses to those who have been trained at aforementioned centers, and some have gone on to employ workers in the local villages, towns and regions. In this regard, BCA-USA has been prominent, followed by the Bakossi Cultural and Development Association and the Mamfe Cultural and Development Association.

However, the question remains as to how long these remittances would last as the 2nd and 3rd generations of Africans in the Diaspora feel less and less emotional connections to the country of their parents' origin over time. The answer, I think, could take either of two directions. If the current rate of emigration out of Africa continues, whether triggered by ecology or economic factors, then there is reason to believe that these remittances would continue, as new immigrants would still have that emotional and familial obligation or still feel the need to help those they left back in their home countries.

On the other hand, if the economic conditions improve and

opportunities to be gainfully employed, either through companies or self-ownership of businesses, then the incentive to emigrate out of the continent would cease to exist, hence dampening transnational movements to settle permanently abroad.

Finally, African governments should recognize the important role that the Diaspora play and could continue to play in poverty reduction and alleviating misery while improving the overall national and continental wellbeing of their compatriots back home. Globalization does not have to be and should not be allowed to mean the abdication of sovereignty.

CHAPTER FIVE

AN IMPORTANT STEP FORWARD

Agriculture and Agribusiness

Africa's path to economic development would, by necessity, go through enhanced agricultural production. Until Africa can feed its burgeoning population, all policy actions toward reducing poverty on the continent would be grossly inadequate. Malnutrition is still a major problem across many countries. The effects range from stunted human growth to brain underdevelopment and related health problems of various types.

Since governments are the key actors, they would have to be proactive in mobilizing the other key stakeholders such as agricultural cooperatives, NGOs involved in both environmental and forestry sectors, and recognized scientific experts in these interrelated fields. Political leadership would have to create room to receive ideas from the civil society organizations and make use of scientific recommendations coming from empirically sound studies and recommendations that are country-specific due to geography and psychographics.

Because of the urgency of this problem, former United Nations Secretary General, Kofi Annan, spearheaded the creation of a think tank called Africa Progress Panel. This coalition comprised former heads of state such as Nigeria's Olusegun Obasanjo and other prominent ex-statesmen across the continent to carry out studies and make policy recommendations to African governments.

Africa, which has 60% of the world's arable land, with up to 600 million hectares of uncultivated land, should not be a net importer of food, but rather, a net exporter. With up to 65% to 72% in some countries of Africa's population involved in agriculture for its livelihood, it makes good economics to invest heavily in this sector. Sadly enough, 80% of Africa's crop production still depends on rainfall, not irrigation. According to UN data, about 239 million Africans are hungry and malnourished - 20 million more in 2015 than four years prior.[25]

It is my contention that there should be a mix of empowering small holder farmers to increase yields and climate resistance seeds via financing, while newer farmlands could be mechanized. Where possible, many smallholder farmers could voluntarily pool their farmlands together and benefit from high tech farming and increased capital and economies of scale.

Not only would this increase production, but equally productivity. The reduced costs and benefits of economies of scale cannot be overemphasized. They could do this and still remain landlords, rather than giving up their family farmlands to foreign multinationals whose sole objective would be profit for both domestic and foreign markets.

Governments should take all necessary measures to invest in road infrastructure and encourage private sector financing in storage facilities and transformative activities. The scheme by the World Bank/IMF and FAO to grab arable lands in Africa must be pointed out and resisted.

In this scheme, developed world governments pressure developing country governments to open up lands to foreign corporations and exempt them from being sued for environmental damages and national appropriations when the terms of contracts are breached by MNCs. African countries must learn and not repeat the mistakes Latin American countries such as Peru, Venezuela and several others did in the 80s and found themselves enslaved by the MNCs.

African governments are capable of resisting these predatory practices and charting development models other than those prescribed by the IMF/WBG, which are essentially sugarcoated but detrimental, economically, environmentally and politically. Turning land-rich peasants into landless tenants is the worst thing that can happen to African countries. This would, if allowed to take hold, set back Africa's real political and economic independence for decades.

Therefore, proactively facilitating access to needed capital for transformative agribusinesses should be one of government's priorities. This would add value, facilitate transportation and transformation, and increase access by the growing consumer base that is swelling the African middle class.

The need to further emphasize the importance of reliable sustainable electricity remains a key component and requirement for the agribusiness enterprises expected to be spawned out of this industry. Jason Miks of CNN warns, "Multinationals should not be allowed to grab all peasant lands and use Africa's natural resources, including water, to produce food for exports while locals starve."[26]

The New Economic Partnership for Development (NEPAD), founded in Lagos in 2002, has equally been active in promoting agriculture as the base for Africa's economic takeoff. NEPAD has had its Climate Smart Agriculture program for some time now and its impact is being felt.

The African Union set Agenda 2063 as the year for Africa to achieve full economic independence and political integration of the entire continental one government, with food sufficiency being attained by 2025. According to its research, Africa will need 4.3 million engineers and 8 million doctors and health experts each year for the foreseeable future. Professor Nnadozie of the African Union recommends that education be reoriented to focus investment in youth, science and technology.[27]

NEPAD also recommends that governments accelerate regional economic integration by creating and reinforcing economic communities with the eventual goal of arriving at a continental single market, single currency and single continental parliament.

This goal and measures were declared in 1991 through the Abuja Treaty, but the results have not been satisfactory. Cross border projects, intra-regional economic development, eliminating visa requirements and other barriers to movement of people and goods and services would greatly accelerate economic opportunities.

When almost half the 55 countries that make up the continent have populations of 10 million and less, pooling resources together and creating a huge borderless market would open a new world of opportunities and enhance poverty reduction measures. Political leaders would have to scale up investment in these sectors intra-regionally.

The almost one third of landlocked African countries stand to benefit more from regional economic integration than working in isolation. According to World Economic Forum's economist,

Catherine KO, "Regional integration can help Africa build value chains, and thereby tap into global value chains."[28]

Energy Provision and Climate Change

According to the UNDP and Africa Progress Panel, 2 in 3 Africans lack access to electricity. The current cost of energy in Sub-Saharan Africa is too high for the 621 million who lack electricity. Halving this cost would make available $5 billion for people living on less than $2.50 a day each year or an additional $36 per household. It has been estimated that approximately $55 billion would be needed each year in energy sector investments to close the energy gap between Sub-Saharan Africa and the rest of the world.

As former United Nations Secretary General, Kofi Annan, puts it, "No region has contributed less to global warming and stands to lose most if the problem of climate change is not addressed, mitigated and resolved." Low carbon future is what would drive Africa's economic development. Africa's stake is huge and requires urgent attention by policy makers.

Investment in low carbon energy sources like solar, geothermal, wind and hydro are strongly encouraged. Political leadership and practical policies could make a difference. The fact that the entire electricity consumption of Sub-Saharan Africa is less than that of Spain is unacceptable but shows the huge existing gap per capita. This should jolt African leaders and the international community into action if there is genuine desire to lift Africa out of poverty.

Other areas to be addressed are waste, inefficiency and corruption in energy production and distribution. It has been estimated that these ills cost 2.4% of Africa's annual GDP. The need is significant—the market of $10 billion a year for investors could place Africa on an accelerated pace toward sustainable development, poverty reduction and higher human development index.

At an investment of $55 billion dollar per year in the energy sector, Africa could conceivably close the current energy gap by year 2030, bringing electricity access to every African. By that date, the continent's population is expected to have hit 2 billion, with about 1 billion in the workforce.

The good news is that some countries, notably Nigeria, South Africa, Ethiopia, Ghana, the Democratic Republic of Congo and

Kenya are already at the forefront of transitioning to low carbon economic drive. Africa's efforts in curbing fossil fuel emissions would have to be matched by a corresponding reduction and elimination of the subsidies that developed world governments give to their companies. Africa is already suffering bigger losses from worldwide emissions and is yet to industrialize.

It would be essential that African countries speak with one voice in demanding real concrete action and implementation by her developed world partners to move from lofty declarations and alluring communiqués that follow each summit on climate change challenges. African countries are yet to understand why the developed countries, through the IMF/WBG, push for a cessation of subsidies to their developing country parastatal corporations while subsidizing their own corporations engaged in the fossil fuel industry. Africa Progress Panel sums up the picture of Africa's energy landscape as such, "Utility reform, new technologies and new business models could be as transformative in energy as the mobile phone was in telecommunication."[29]

One new area that could be explored in addition to the plenty of sunshine for solar is sand. Energy could be tapped from sand, and Africa has some of the world's largest deserts, notably the Sahara - the world's largest at 3.3 million square miles. Moreover, covering 25% of the continent, the Namib and the Kalahari, almost evenly placed by God across the continental landmass, make grid and transportation much easier.

Some inspiration could be gotten from how energy from desert sand is being tapped in the United Arab Emirates. Also, solar on a mass scale could be learned from the fellow African country of Morocco, even though it has not been part of the African Union for the past three decades, but recently was readmitted in 2016 upon demand.

With sufficient energy, Africa could feed itself and still have food for export. Kofi Annan put it best with his proposal—triple wins, which are: available agricultural productivity, climate change, and climate mitigation. Renewable technologies can create opportunities for increased productivity and long-term carbon mitigation.

Before the Climate Summit held in Paris in December 2015, grouping all 183 UN member states and more (195 countries signed the final document), African countries were going to the annual summit to steer negotiations away from the stale "common but differentiated responsibilities" to "equitable access to sustainable development."[30] They were to push for increased climate change financing, among other priorities. Currently, many African countries are spending more of their scarce financial resources to meet the United Nations Framework Convention on Climate Change (UNFCCC) guidelines in meeting the low carbon levels than they receive from the Climate Change financing. Nigeria, Ethiopia are good examples. The latest action by President Trump withdrawing America from the Climate Summit means that the developing countries that had hoped to be compensated by America's pledge of financial support might not meet the agreed upon less than 2.0c emissions.

The Intended Nationally Determined Contributions (INDCs) provide African governments with a vehicle to set out their transition to a growth oriented, climate resilient, low carbon development model. African policy makers and stakeholders must realize that they need to gradually abandon fossil fuel energy to green technology sources if they hope to forestall reversals made during the last two decades in agriculture, industry and socioeconomic development.

The INDCs are guidelines and thresholds that were decided upon at the Warsaw Climate Summit in 2013, which called upon every country to adopt a set of measures to reduce emissions by 2015 and for each country to submit its own target and progress report. It is a set of policies by governments which measure, both quantitatively and qualitatively, emissions from greenhouse gases to the United Nations Framework Convention on Climate Change (UN FCCC) secretariat for review. These help a country plan to develop economically in a sustainable manner while reducing greenhouse gases and applying mitigation measures.

The 2015 Paris Climate Summit: Results

The Paris Climate Change Summit held in Paris in December 2015 saw some progress as well as some setbacks, as was expected. While one may say it was a step forward by the international community to continue tackling global warming caused by emissions from fossil fuel usage, in some respects the outcome fell short of Africa's expectations, especially Sub-Saharan Africa.

Some positives of the Summit included goals in Article 1 such as commitment by all countries to reduce emissions to 1.5c from the 2.0c that had been set in Copenhagen earlier in 2014. The problem here, as expected, was that the measures in place designed to force countries into compliance were non-punitive. They simply urged governments to pursue efforts meant to reduce emissions.

About 180 countries had submitted their INDCs, but the vague wording meant that some countries could, due to economic pressures, go even higher than the 2.0c threshold. Countries were "invited to" but not asked to "strive to" achieve lower carbon footprints in their development drive, resulting in lack of compliance and accountability.

Other Articles, such as 14, required that country review takes place every five years. Article 8, in particular, was the turning point as the US delegation argued against compensation for damages caused by multinationals, and this article was watered down in the hopes of having the US Senate approve it. With the Senate led by Republicans who repeatedly deny climate change and global warming, one cannot predict the outcome when these articles are presented by the Obama administration for ratification. The updated information is that, as feared, the new US president has withdrawn the US from the Paris Summit.

Article 9, which calls for continuing finance for climate change to help developing countries, has now changed as the $100 billion per year from the developed countries to their developing counterparts is concerned. Article 7 called for the establishment of global goals on adaptation of "enhancing adaptation capacity, strengthening resilience and reducing vulnerability to climate change."[31]

Countries must periodically submit their adaptation planning for review. The 195 countries that finally signed onto the broad goal of achieving low carbon sustainable economic development agreed to shift from fossil fuels to renewables by the end of the second half of the 21st century.

Critic, Jesse Moore, says, "The agreement will ensure that the developing countries bear the cost because using deficit financing to subsidize uneconomic technologies will expand government balance sheets at a time of already ballooning budgets and debt that will affect all markets and industries in the future."[32]

He has a point there, given the debt burden in loan servicing that most developing countries are facing amid growing demand for social services and other human development investments that cannot be neglected. Developing countries face the added dilemma of not having the technical know-how in measuring the greenhouse gas emissions and presenting to the Secretariat for review.

CHAPTER SIX

THE WAY FORWARD 2:1

Political Infrastructure

If there is one overarching factor that affects all other facets of societal life and every citizen, it is politics. It is critically important that politics takes an all new meaning because of the way it permeates African countries. Earlier, we touched on this subject, tracing today's development challenges to the type of political and administrative systems that the ex-colonial powers of Europe put into place.

There is little argument that the West built political foundations that were designed to fail over time and could not be sustainable. They were, from the outset, prone to disputes, conflicts, political instability and generalized insecurity. Inherently conflictual as these political foundations were, ignorance and man's proclivity to greed exacerbated these deficiencies, and millions of African lives have been lost as a result of fratricidal wars, both international and intra-African.

Millions more have been displaced and made refugees in other more stable countries across the continent. Some countries, such as the Democratic Republic of Congo, have been on perpetual war footing for more than a decade. Sudan was in a similar situation for over three decades. Angola was not spared either, nor was Africa's largest country, Nigeria, which saw a bloody civil war and many military coups d'état.

It is against this backdrop that a better understanding of the role of politics in Africa's economic development would be situated. The post-independence era was characterized by strong men leading one party polities full of weak institutions. The artificial carving up of natural frontiers that separated homogenous peoples brought about deep resentment among and between people who had little to nothing in common, either culturally, geographically, religiously or politically. Political kingdoms with well-structured systems existed before the arrival of the colonizers from Europe.

Since political independence in the late fifties and early sixties, most of those who took over power from the Europeans were, and remain, authoritarian. Today, more than half of the 55 African countries are ruled by authoritarian regimes. Even in countries where democratic elections have been organized, the casting of ballots by voters has not resulted in change in power. In a majority of cases, the president has total control over the election boards, ministry or authority, while being the chief magistrate in the judicial system in addition to his role as commander-in-chief of the armed forces. They hide behind the name democracy to rule with iron fist using the military as the coercive force to guarantee their staying power. Simply stated, most African nations are ruled by the military headed by civilian presidents.

Except in some English-speaking African countries, most French-speaking ex-colonies of France have the strong man appointing all regional or provincial governors, mayors and, of course, cabinet ministers and managers of parastatal corporations. It is evident from the above that this kind of system cannot, and has not bode well for societal development as the patronage system—tribalism, nepotism, endemic and systemic corruption and lack of accountability still reign supreme.

Some of these dictators have perfected their polities to the extent that everyone is ready to settle scores with perceived and real rivals/enemies by serving as unsolicited informants/spies to the incumbent regimes. Intellectuals and university professors vie to leave their classrooms and research laboratories to become administrators and run budgets out of which they would siphon off a huge percentage for their personal and family use. Concepts such as good governance and accountability are anathema to the ears of these officials.

Entry into all professional schools, including medical schools, are more often than not determined by which candidate's parents can afford the exorbitant bribe sums, versus by competence and performance on the competitive entrance exams. In this atmosphere, all competitive exams become a charade. Officials at every level curry favors with those at the top by literally slashing an important portion of the state allocated investment and functional/operations budget back to the ministerial and/or departmental bosses. These practices ensure that they maintain their posts for as long as they can continue feeding the top layers of officials.

The long-term consequences of these malevolent practices are disastrous for the economy on every front. In such systems, the poorer get poorer as funds leave the bottom to the top political elites, administrators and functionaries. Healthcare suffers, education of youth suffers, investments in infrastructural development—programs and projects—seldom get off the ground, and for those that do, they sooner than later fall apart and the cycle of underdevelopment is accentuated.

Retrogression sets in and the combination of inefficiently allocated resources and labor results in stagnation. Productivity becomes a forlorn goal as relevant skills and talents become harder to find, leading to a decline in aggregate output in the economy. The nation borrows more from the International Financial Institutions (IFIs) with all their draconian conditionality, and debt servicing continues to have its own bite, draining whatever scarce financial resources the nations have left.

Current leaders of African countries would be better off establishing stronger national institutions and inculcating a political culture that recognizes and respects institutions more than office holders who are ephemeral. Democratic institutions codified in strong constitutions able to withstand shocks and crises are some of the political reforms needed for sustained development.

Currently, only a few countries such as South Africa, Kenya, Ghana, Rwanda and Nigeria are taking steps to reinforce this political culture. Independent electoral commissions and independent judiciary are some key pillars of democracy. Partially free press, jointly funded by private capital and public funds, are essential to maintaining a balance of coverage.

Until term limits are instituted and respected by each and every citizen, there could still be problems. The military should be trained and educated to keep out of politics and be subordinate to civilian control and authority. The role of the military should be well defined and taught at schools, stressing their duty to protect the national territory and institutions, not just the executive branch which in many cases are headed by a tribesman.

Too many African militaries have been coopted to serve the interests of the president and his perpetuity in power. This must change. The military should be professionalized and well paid to dissuade its officers from ever dreaming of taking over political power by force of arms. Rule of law and respect for human rights should be codified and disseminated across every nation and taught in civics classes at schools of all levels.

The Agenda 2063 that was proclaimed at the 50th anniversary commemorations of the founding of the Organization of African Unity in Addis Ababa—forerunner to the African Union and the vision of the founding fathers—is a noble goal. To build on the ambitious goals of that vision and mission, the value of that vision should be taught from elementary schools in each of the 55 countries that make up the African Union.

One of its key preambles is "United in Diversity, sharing a common culture and looking forward to having shared prosperity." If this schooling is not begun early, tomorrow's African leaders—today's youth—would be hard pressed to see themselves as one people with a common destiny. Political and economic integration of the continent could remain a distant and forlorn aspiration—an elusive goal.

Economic Development Model and Reform

As earlier stated, the colonial powers who carved out Africa without regard to linguistic, cultural or geographic considerations, made economic development of disparate peoples a very onerous task. Even the post-independence structures were ill-fitted for any meaningful development, much less sustainable development. Africa's importance to the West was limited to supplying the raw materials meant to feed industries in the Western countries.

This practice went on for a century until China rose and entered the scene, offering a different economic development model. Unlike the so-called Washington Consensus, which emphasized economic development through private capital and free market system, having as a necessary corollary of political rights with less nationalism, the Chinese model was markedly different. It emphasized national sovereignty over resources and economic rights, or what some have dubbed "right to bread" over less individual political or human rights.

The Chinese model holds that economic rights should be at par in importance with human political rights. They argue that a country as vast and populated like theirs could never have attained the level of societal transformation from an agrarian backward country, less than six decades ago into a modern world economic superpower it is today without adopting this model.

Many African intellectuals and scholars of development find these arguments persuasive with regards to the vast continent of Africa that aspires to become a major global economic and political power. The memory of the West's neglect in the aftermath of slavery, colonialism, apartheid, subjugation and neocolonialism has tilted the African's thought more toward the Chinese model of economic development and less toward the Washington or Western model. They have plenty of evidence to support the Chinese model.

For one, the Washington Consensus is based on the World Bank/IMF economic development model, which, among other conditions, emphasizes the role of the private sector, deregulation, elimination of subsidies to state enterprises, and protection of multinational corporations.

Additionally, African leaders and development scholars are suspicious of the Washington model, especially as concerns its insistence on eliminating all national laws that forbid foreign corporate ownership of land. Also, they are wary of immunity from suits against MNCs from damages caused to local communities, such as environmental pollution, forest over-exploitation and organized labor union rights. The case and struggle of Nigeria's Niger Delta Ogoni people against the energy giant Shell oil and the assassination of Ken Saro-Wiwa are well documented as these people fight the pollution of their water resources and land by oil spills and neglect.

The case of Peru in the early 90s is a glaring and compelling example. When Peru came under the IMF/WBG Structural Adjustment Program, the promised higher human development index that was to have emanated from poverty alleviation reforms left a sour taste for millions of indigenous people.

Their lands were expropriated by American MNCs for logging, mining and deforestation. Water pollution from pesticides killed soil and children and destroyed their sources of livelihoods. Drilling and oil spills left the lands and water dead and unfit for human habitation. These reforms led to previous land owners becoming landless farm workers. Conflicts, illnesses and other health care issues caused by land grab and irresponsible exploitation accentuated poverty and triggered social distress, unrest and misery instead.

Peru's case, as well as many others in Latin America and Africa, has been well documented by the Oakland Institute. Cameroon's Pygmies in the forest regions stand out as another bad case where logging and other agro-industrial activities have not contributed to the wellbeing of riverine peoples.

It is for these and many other related reasons that the African managers of Africa's modernization process are increasingly opting for the Chinese economic development model. The proponents of this model further argue that a hungry man or a multitude of hungry people would be more interested in food sufficiency than in some human or political rights, which they argue could and should come later. Food security and the provision of basic needs such as potable water, electricity, health and education trump human rights as premier human needs.

The African Union's Agenda 2063, which is an all-inclusive, comprehensive document, stands as a veritable blueprint that would leapfrog the continent forward to close the development gap with the rest of the world. It contains aspects of these two models without explicitly delineating the tenets or underpinnings of each one.

While not being the subject of this book, it might suffice to mention Agenda 2063 here. To briefly sum it up, it is a visionary blueprint Solemn Declaration Document that contains 71 detailed goals, purposes and guidelines, grouped under seven broad comprehensive aspirations that are expected to be realized continent-wide by the year 2063.

Despite this solemn declaration, there is ongoing debate as to which socioeconomic development model Africa should adopt. This debate is not only important, but urgent and necessary. Lead economist, Simplice A. Asongu, from the research department of the African Governance and Development Institute, suggests a merger of the two development models. In his view, Africa should adopt what he calls "the middle passage." He states inter alia, "...with an approach that merges the Chinese and Western models—balancing human rights with national economic interests."[33]

Reflecting along a similar vein, B. R. Ambedkar champions

economic rights of citizens to live a decent and dignified life when he states, "…even the fundamental rights given to citizens are of no use to the have-nots in the absence of social and economic equality and opportunity."[34] The latter gentleman was speaking about the much touted Millennium Development Goals that the UN had set at the beginning of this 21st century to be achieved by 2015, which most countries have failed to attain to date.

If African countries enhance individual rights with sovereign authority and political rights with economic goals, their development goals would be considerably advanced. I am of the view that this middle passage would be best for Africa, given that different countries are endowed differently, whether we are discussing natural or human resources.

Geography and maritime resources differ across countries, and these are all assets for continent-wide development. It would also leave room to adopt best practices from member states that have efficiently applied them. Proven and productive practices that meet human needs and contributes to poverty reduction, higher life expectancy, and higher human development index should be pursued.

If Africa, as one national entity in construction, truly wants to succeed while participating in world affairs, it must make it clear to the West, in particular, and to the rest of the world, that henceforth, Africa's natural resources would not be taken by force of arms or by those who have a mistaken presumption of entitlement. Africa's 1.2 billion plus people have inalienable rights to their natural resources, and the time has come to end the continuation of feeding the wellbeing of Western nations to the detriment of these indigenous people.

Food Security in Africa

The challenge of food insecurity in many countries across the continent is a perennial problem that needs urgent attention. Africa suffers from food and malnutrition issues due to a number of factors that range from climatic, e.g. drought, to institutional, political and intra-national conflicts. As we observed earlier in a previous chapter, Africa accounts for 60% of the world's arable land, yet it remains a net importer of food for millions of its people.

Despite pledges and commitments by governments to increase investment in agriculture, only a few countries have been able to meet the minimum threshold of 10% of national budgets devoted to this key sector set by NEPAD's Comprehensive Africa Agriculture Development Program, or CAADP, which is a policy framework for agricultural development in Africa for the 21st century. It is aimed at, among other directives contained therein, ensuring food security and sufficiency in Africa by 2025, starting in 2015.

Food security has been defined by the Food and Agricultural Organization (FAO) as access to a quantity and quality of food sufficient for everyone to live a healthy and decent life (FAO, 1996). However, food security as a concept has evolved over the years to transcend food sufficiency to people's right to access adequate and nutritious food (Le Schutter, 2010).[35]

This rights-based approach focuses attention on the more naturally vulnerable segments of society, such as women and children. It supports basic human rights to food and equates this fundamental need with other human rights. When governments fail to do everything in their power to ensure this basic right, they should be held accountable for violation.

Another addition to the concept of food security is what Rosset (2008) and Wittman (2009)[36] have dubbed "Food Sovereignty." Simply stated, they advocate that the local people have a say over food production and for whom food is produced, as cited in ACBF Occasional Paper 23. If African governments fully implement the required actions contained in the CAADP and reaffirmed at the 2014 Malabo Declaration on accelerated agricultural growth, Africa could be on her way to ensuring meaningful food security for all her citizens while still retaining plenty for export by 2025.

A current source of a potentially disturbing phenomenon is the land grabbing that is taking place in many countries on the continent. According to Cotula (2012),[37] between 2008 and 2010, African countries sold about 63 million hectares of farmlands to MNCs/TNCs. These countries included Nigeria, Madagascar, Ethiopia, Mali, Sudan and Mozambique.

The risk in selling farmlands to TNCs is the tendency of these corporations to produce mostly cash crops like palm oil, rubber, coffee, tea, cocoa for export markets and ignoring food crops like corn, beans, cereal, beets, tuber crops, potatoes and tomatoes. Some African countries, like Nigeria, need to import up to 1.8 million metric tons of tomatoes to make up for the 2.3 million metric tons needed for domestic consumption at the colossal price tag of over $1 billion annually.

Compounding this shortfall is the 50% that is lost due to poor storage, processing and transportation difficulties. There are still no guarantees that these corporations would produce food for domestic markets, since external markets might be more profitable. According to FAO data, more than 20 million Africans are undernourished in the Horn of Africa (FAO, 2010).[38]

In response to this trend, I recommend that farmlands should not be leased to TNCs for more than 30-year periods like the government of Cameroon did with a French agro-industrial company for a dumbfounding 60 years.

CHAPTER SEVEN

African Investors and Innovators

Today, African youth are beginning to see innovation and investment as the keys to the continent's socioeconomic development, which is an encouraging trend. African youth are more business savvy, possessing an entrepreneurial spirit that would drive innovation in industrialization across the continent. They are increasingly manifesting a penchant for savings and investment.

Therefore, innovation, as an important transformative tool to economic development, must be encouraged by policy makers. It engenders wealth creation by developing new products and processes of supply chain management. It creates jobs as more people use these products to solve existing practical problems.

Moreover, it is widely understood that information technologies, when applied to manufacturing, transportation and market access, create more job opportunities. E-commerce is growing geometrically across the continent and generating supply chain jobs.

As governments across the continent strive to implement Agenda 2063, political, civil society leaders and business community leaders must periodically convene regional conventions that would review progress, correct errors made, and make necessary adjustments moving forward. These reviews would be useful to measure target attainment using previously established structural benchmarks.

A World Bank survey on October 14, 2014 of 7,000 African youth from about eleven countries, mostly from Southern and Eastern Africa, found that 49% of respondents indicated that they would save 50% if given $100 USD. In addition, they pointed out that they would invest in education, computers and books.[39]

These are encouraging signs as the expected growth of the middle class across Africa would impact innovation and investment in sectors that produce the needed goods and services to meet growing demand. Governments across the continent would be better advised to create enabling environments within their countries, within which these dynamic rising class of innovators and investors could thrive.

A select area that would drive growth and development is digital renaissance. Electronic payment is booming and has contributed to the rapid economic growth over the past decade as urbanization has leapfrogged. According to Forbes, consumer spending is expected to exceed $411 billion annually by 2020.[40]

This growth, emanating from population increase, would by itself, result in higher demand for residential and commercial real estate. Demand for modern office space is on the rise in urban areas, and this demand would also spur the growth in information and communications technology (ICT).

Companies such as MTN, Tigo, Airtel and M-Pesa are already in the driver's seat and it is expected that more companies will enter the industry in the years to come. With the exception of MTN, most of these companies operate in the East African Economic Community. Kenya, which has been the world's third fastest growing economy behind only China and the Philippines, is the seat of tech growth in Africa. Its workforce is highly educated and its investment climate attractive, with roughly 60% of its population aged 25 and younger (University of Michigan's William Davidson Institute, 2015).[41]

Another great driver of the continent's economic renaissance is Nigeria, which, according to *The Economist*, boasted around 7% growth during the past decade and bypassed South Africa as Africa's largest economy. The entire continent of Africa is expected to continue this kind of impressive economic growth of around 5% annually during this decade. According the World Bank's Africa Pulse, published in 2013, consumer spending was responsible for over 60% of Sub-Saharan economic growth.

At the expected 5% annual growth, this would still be higher than the world average. The African Development Bank contends that approximately 123 million Africans can be considered middle class, representing about 13% of the continent's current population. Should this trend continue, by 2060, this number could reach 1.1 billion.

As earlier stated, the implications are many. If policy makers manage this growth in population and urbanization well, Africa could attain the dreams of the founding fathers of the OAU, now the African Union, as espoused in Agenda 2063, which strive for a strong, integrated continental Africa, both politically and economically.

Achieving these goals would require huge investments in infrastructure. It is worth repeating that investments would need to be directed to infrastructure—roads, railways, port facilities, power generation, telecommunications, and education, with emphasis on science, technology, engineering and mathematics (STEM).

Also noteworthy is the fact that 90% of trade between African countries is by sea, which is one reason part of Agenda 2063 placed a high premium on Africa's "Blue Economy." Again, Kenya is taking the lead here. The country is expected to invest around $55.6 billion in improvements in the above cited sectors. I strongly call upon other African countries to follow Kenya's lead.

The good news is that Ethiopia, Uganda, Tanzania, Nigeria, Botswana and, of course, South Africa, are making headways. Ghana and Egypt are also expected to take these developments seriously. Cameroon organized an international investment conference in May 2016, geared toward attracting venture capitalists and encouraging domestic innovators.

Most of the participants were former heads of such organizations as the World Bank, World Trade Organization and the United Nations Development Program. Also expected in attendance was Africa's richest man and 105th wealthiest in the world, Nigeria's Aliko Dangote.

The World Bank estimates that there are about 90 startup hubs across Africa encouraging diversification by investors and venture capitalists who could reduce risks and increase reward. This model of "investing wide" as opposed to "investing deep" is seen by investors as advantageous.

Again, this is where bringing down physical and trade barriers between countries would propel economic development across the continent. The elimination of tariffs, customs duties, visa requirements between countries and regions would only serve as a catalyst to the attainment of a strong and united African economic superpower—One Africa.

In 2014, trade among African countries was 18%, compared to 65% for Europe, 52% for Asia, and 50% for North America (World

Economic Forum, 2015).[42] As aforementioned, African Youth are more educated, more tech savvy, more inclined to business startups, and more interconnected.

Furthermore, these millennials are hungry for change, innovations and a better standard of living. These new crops of young entrepreneurs are teeming with enthusiasm, energy and ambition. They represent the future of Africa and must be invited to the table. They must be given their own space to innovatively transform societies in Africa.

There is a growing trend in Africa where young Africans are developing technologies for use in solving existing problems in Africa. For many decades, Africa, which has been a net consumer and importer of technologies, is beginning to reduce and reverse that old practice.

For example, a millennial from Cameroon by the name Arthur Zang, has developed a mobile EKG handheld medical device that would serve the populations in rural areas by rapidly transmitting electrocardiogram results to city-based doctors for rapid intervention to save lives. There are thousands like him across the continent who are yet to come into the limelight.

Africa is chronically underwired, and this problem, in itself, presents a huge opportunity for venture capitalists to fill the gap and satisfy the huge and growing demand. Any attempt at shutting out entrepreneurial millennials would only retard growth and socioeconomic development, as well as negatively impact national and continental wellbeing.

Truth be told, it would be bad policy for Africa's political leadership to ignore this ambitious group. Not only must they be given a seat at the table, but smart policymakers would do better by supporting these young entrepreneurs with funding. South Africa's Cape Town and Durban, Ethiopia and Angola, are doing just that.

Those countries in Africa that create legal frameworks and attractive, actionable investment codes shall be the ones that would see the rush of venture capitalists, whether they be domestic or foreign. The technology sector will remain one of the key drivers of Africa's economic takeoff. This sector could benefit from encouraging the STEM subjects. These tools represent the future equally, if more millennials put them to use in e-commerce, market information, and supply chain and distribution.

The internet penetration rate in the continent, while being low, is poised to increase, and the higher the internet penetration rate of a country, the greater the GDP and income. So far, Nigeria has proven that increased application of internet technology and connectivity can increase aggregate GDP, jobs and national wellbeing. This is one of the factors that led Nigeria's economy to bypass South Africa's to become Africa's largest economy at US$500 billion in 2014. Unfortunately for 2015 and 2016, growth declined due to drop in oil prices and a slump in demand for commodities as China's demand and growth slowed. That giant nation's economy grew by 2.7% in 2015 dropping from 6.3 a year earlier in 2014. A negative -1.8 % growth was registered in 2016 (IMF World Economic Outlook 2016).[43]

From my perspective, I do not see any conflicts or contradictions between encouraging private sector development with government control and regulatory framework to protect nascent domestic industries. Unbridled capitalism has proven disastrous in the US, with growing discontent due to income and wealth disparities, while heavy government control on the economy, such as in Zimbabwe, has negated economic development.

It is with this backdrop that I strongly recommend the "Middle Passage" model of economic development, featuring a judicious mix of the Washington Consensus, or Western Model, with the Chinese Economic Model.

CHAPTER EIGHT

RECOMMENDATIONS AND PROGNOSIS

As we have seen throughout the preceding chapters of this book, Africa's turn at real economic development has come. It has not been by accident either, but by a combination of conscious leadership desire to lift the continent out of lethargy, inertia, ridicule, under-development; and the world economic evolution. Africa's image in the world has been marred by negative news such as famine, wars, poverty and misery.

While famine has had some of its root causes in wars and frat-ricidal conflicts, drought has also significantly resulted in periodic low crop yields in certain parts of Africa. The Sahel region readily comes to mind. These causal factors have also seen mass emigration and internal displacements of affected people in the millions. It is these and other factors that jolted some African leaders to revive the dreams of the founding fathers of the OAU.

Gathering in Addis Ababa in April 2001, it was decided to transform the OAU into the African Union, to begin moving the continent from a region that supplied the raw materials for the industries of Europe and the wellbeing of the West to Afrocentric development. This Africa first and Africa-centered developmental shift was lauded by many on the continent and in the diaspora.

Despite the slow pace of the process of economic and political integration agreed upon by various heads of state at African summits over the decades, progress has been registered on many fronts. Many challenges lie ahead, but the past decade has witnessed impres-sive economic growth and economic development within certain countries. Over the past decade, six out of the ten fastest growing economies in the world have been in Africa, where average annual GDP has hovered around 5.6 percent.

Challenges linger in political and economic reforms,

infrastructural implantation, energy or power generation, regional economic integration, road networks linking all countries in the continent, railways and port facilities, and education tailored for societal transformation.

However, if African leaders work diligently and in unity, the goals, the aspirations and objectives of Agenda 2063 would become a reality. The realization of these noble goals would be undertaken largely, but not exclusively by Africans alone. Africa's willing development partners would also play an important role in technical assistance such as capacity building and funding.

The attainment of these aspirations and goals would be facilitated by three major assets available to the continent:

1. Large population with inbuilt large internal market. By 2050, Africa's population would be over 3 billion people with 1.8 billion baby births expected over the next 35 years (UNICEF 2014).[44] By 2100, 39%, or about 4 billion of the projected global population of 11.2 billion people on the planet will be in Africa.

2. Almost unlimited, abundant natural resources—arable land, minerals and forests, and blue economic resources i.e. water, to serve industrialization and manufacturing transformation. There is also abundant sunshine for solar, sand, hydropower potential, wind and geothermal energy to power African homes, institutions and industries.

3. Over one billion work force with about three quarters being urban dwellers across a huge landmass by 2050. According to Bloomberg Report, by 2035 Africa alone will have added more people to the workforce than the rest of the world combined.[45]

As impressive as these statistics and data are, the challenges to leadership to harness these enormous human and natural resources for sustainable socioeconomic development would be daunting.

On the flip side, however, these challenges in demographic explosion and urbanization are equally attractive opportunities for GDP growth and higher human development index. These present rewarding opportunities to entrepreneurs to avail themselves of and to provide solutions to these needs.

This also means that African political leadership would have to move from rhetoric and declarations of political will to proactive policy actions. With youth population across the continent growing fast, Africa's leaders would have to invest in education that emphasizes in-demand skillsets to enter industry, create jobs as entrepreneurs and forge viable productive partnerships.

Internet Penetration

Africa lags far behind the rest of the world in internet connectivity. Data shows that countries with greater internet usage are better off economically than those with lower penetration. Information, Communication and Technology, or ICT, has become an indispensable tool for development, business and modern life. With the internet, information can be easily communicated to farmers on available markets, types, weather conditions, logistics and transportation, distribution, just to name a few.

As a result, business decision-making can be carried out in a timely manner, thus saving unnecessary costs and delays across thousands of miles. E-commerce cannot function without internet, nor can electronic payments and processing. Therefore, the importance of internet access and connectivity in economic development cannot be overemphasized.

In the continent, the average rate of penetration is 26.8% compared to the world average of 50%. Nigeria leads the continent in internet connectivity and usage in business at 92%, followed by Egypt at 48.3%, Kenya at 31.9% and South Africa at 26.8%.

I think that Nigeria's widespread use of internet was one of the key contributory factors to its overtaking South Africa to become Africa's largest economy. Moreover, I observed a pattern in the continent on internet usage I find noteworthy: of the top ten countries with highest internet connectivity, eight are English-speaking with only two - Morocco in 5th place and Tunisia in 10th place, which are both French and Arabic-speaking countries (Internet World Stats, 2015). This observation appears to be consistent with other sectoral comparisons such as the Economic Community of Central African States (ECCAS), which lag behind other regional African economic blocs like ECOWAS, COMESA and SADC.

There seems to be a contrast between heavily centralized

French-speaking Sub-Saharan Africa and English-speaking countries and the speed of progress. The latter are making faster economic progress than the former. Again, this goes to underscore my earlier contention that the centralized less democratic African countries, with the exception of Cote d'Ivoire and Senegal, lag behind their English-speaking counterparts.

Internet fuels trade. Savvy entrepreneurs are using it to increase their bottom line. Google's Africa Connected and Nigeria's Konga are unlocking the power of internet in driving business potential in some countries. These are positive trends and should be encouraged by national leaders if they truly want a strong, united and prosperous Africa capable of playing globally in various fields. The stakes are high and the resources abundant, but action is needed to attain identified goals of moving Africa forward into becoming a modern, developed continent.

Consumer Driven Continental Integration

In almost every publication, whether from the World Bank, United Nations Development Program, International Labor Organization, Organization for Economic Co-operation and Development, Oxfam, or African Development Bank, one common thread is the recognition that Africa is the next frontier for investment, wealth creation, and economic growth and development.

There is also agreement among all observers of Africa's progress that the push factor driving the continent's economy is the rising middle class, especially its millennials, who are well-educated, computer and business savvy, and internet interconnected.

The middle class is a force that has overtaken the policy decision-makers at national levels who are foot-dragging to achieve continental integration. The burgeoning middle class full of millennials are using technology to move faster than politicians as they trade and conduct business across borders that are virtually borderless.

According to renowned philanthropist, Mo Ibrahim, telecommunications and financial services are two sectors where innovation is so fast and all-embracing that it has rendered national restrictions on cross border businesses virtually redundant. New services are being offered much faster than old regulations can cope.

However, while these developments are laudable and should be encouraged, economic integration would not take firm hold without governments able or willing to building roads and railways, air transportation and port infrastructure linking countries to move goods and people.

Comparative advantages in production and trade, as well as economies of scale, would be impossible without these indispensable infrastructural investments. As an example, it does not make any economic sense for Kenya to import some of its needed goods from Europe or far-off America when it could get these goods cheaper and faster from neighboring Tanzania or even from Ghana.

The urgent need to pay greater attention to intra-regional African economic linkages and integration is clear. The 2016 World Economic Forum took place from May 11 to May 13, 2016 in Kigali, the capital of Rwanda, and while it was expected to tackle basketful laundry of the world's multifarious problems, it was an opportunity to showcase some achievements on the rising continent.

Education in STEM

For too long, many African countries ran school and university curricula that had nothing to do with the subjects that create wealth and transform societies. The school systems promoted by the departing colonial powers were detrimental to Africa's socioeconomic development in all facets.

Mathematics and the sciences, whether physical or natural, were not particularly encouraged. Yet, a cursory look across the globe, and specifically Asia, during the last four decades would readily prove that that region's rapid economic growth and development can be credited to emphasis laid on STEM subjects.

Unfortunately, in many African post-independent countries, subjects such as English and French Literature, Poetry and Arts and Religion were priorities in the curricula. Without meaning to offend their scholars, these subjects contribute very little to nothing in societal modernization. History is important only in so far as it could be used to understand the past, modify the present, and shape a better future.

The importance of these subjects has been further validated by the US Congress which recently passed an immigration law that encourages foreign students to stay and work in America for up to three years after graduation if they studied any of the STEM subjects. This is for a country whose national mood is not immigrant friendly (USCIS June 2016).[46]

Once the policy makers across South East Asia, and later China, understood the secret to Western economic dominance and mastered the STEM subjects, their region of the world leapfrogged from backward, largely agrarian societies to modern, industrialized countries. Their economic growth was so high and sustained for so long that they were dubbed "the economic miracles of the Five SE Asian Dragons" in development literature.

Today, China has overtaken the United States as the world's largest economy as measured in PPP or purchasing power parity while the US beats China's economy when measured in nominal GDP (IMF 2016 Stats).[47] Countries such as South Korea, Singapore and Malaysia are competing with OECD countries in many fields of human endeavor without any complex.

For such similar societal transformation to occur in Africa, it would require that governments on the continent facilitate competition and investment in STEM subjects. The public sector alone cannot adequately provide all the capital that would be needed in these sectors, hence the need to promote competition in telecommunications and power or energy production and distribution. Knocking down physical barriers would open investment opportunities, scaling up rewards, creating jobs, and expanding the tax base.

Once the internal markets are enlarged, economies of scale through comparative advantages would be attendant corollaries. The expanded internal African market would then serve as a veritable platform for growth, and pull in more venture capitalists and young, bright entrepreneurs.

Poles of Development and Hubs of Technological Progress

The centrality of Africa in world affairs and consequently, its importance, cannot be underestimated. Given the continent's abundant resources, which after a century or more of exploitation to feed Western industrial needs, is not yet depleted, its arable land that constitutes 60% of the world total, numerous minerals and precious stones, including diamond, gold, columbite—tantalite or coltan, manganese, cobalt and bauxite, to name a few, not to mention hydrocarbons and coal, Africa has a promising future.

Therefore, I contend that the capital cities of present day nations that make up the African Union could serve as poles for economic and technological development going forward. Once the Agenda 2063 has been realized, and even well before that date, the tasks of national governments would be to direct investments and resource allocations to the regions in a decentralized system, politically and administratively.

According to the World Bank, Africa currently has about 117 tech hubs spread across the continent. These tech hubs contain incubators for the digital renaissance of the continent. Most of these tech hubs for mobile telephone users that currently number 700 million subscribers are developed locally, as are the applications. Also, an overwhelming majority of centers for techies, entrepreneurs, millennials, students and journalists interested in tech issues are civil society led. Out of the 117 tech hubs, only ten are government led while 79 are civil society led, with 19 being led by academic institutions and 9 being hybrid government and civil society.[48]

This, and other trends, point to a promising future for Africa as these centers are expected to produce the creative minds that would lead innovation and transform Africa into a major global economic power capable of ensuring food security, affordable and decent healthcare, and access to electricity, portable water and quality education for all African citizens.

As earlier stated, I have observed that most of these tech hubs are in the capital cities, with few exceptions such as Cameroon, where they are civil society led and located outside the capital city and the major economic center of that country. South Africa, for obvious reasons, has the largest number of tech hubs—24, followed by Nigeria and Kenya with 11 each, and Ghana, Egypt and Uganda with 9, 8 and 7, respectively. Senegal, Morocco and Cote d'Ivoire share 5 and 4 each, respectively. The rest of Africa have 2 or 1. It is just ideal and practical that these tech hubs be in or near capital cities and major urban centers out of which many businesses operate.

Furthermore, the current poles of development would radiate outward into the hinterlands as the modernization process is carried forward. A judicious mix of incentives to reward innovation and entrepreneurship and penalties for collusion to fix prices to the detriment of the final consumers by companies would need strict enforcement mechanisms. Decentralized decision-making shall go hand-in-hand with recognition of icons across the continent.

To create a common sense of belonging, leaders or permanent national and continental commissions would be in place to identify and recommend for the naming of icons in countries other than those that produced those icons.

If progress is accelerated as is expected, there has to come a time, sooner than later, when the continent's youth would not see the need to emigrate out of Africa for Europe and North America for economic and educational opportunities. Many Africans have perished in the Sahara Desert and at sea while trying to cross over into Europe. Many have equally been enslaved in some Middle Eastern Arab countries. Poor governance and chronic shortages of opportunities have led to what some have called modern day Africans begging at the borders of Europe to be enslaved. This cannot continue if the determination of weaning Africa from neocolonialism is to be achieved.

Others still, have found themselves in far-off lands such as Thailand, South Korea, Malaysia and Indonesia, where they have suffered discrimination and been beaten to death just for being Africans. These humiliations would cease once the fruits of African Renaissance begin to be harvested.

For over two decades, Africa has lost a significant number of its youth to Europe and America in the name of seeking better opportunities. In the decade of the 90s, the UN reported that about 65% of African youth between the ages of 17 and 35 were actively seeking to leave Africa.

It is therefore incumbent upon today's political leadership across Africa to foster all the agreements emanating from African Union summits in pushing for the implementation of Agenda 2063. It behooves all Africans, especially political leaders, to continue on the work that the Founding Fathers of the OAU began and died fighting for.

If they pick up the mantle, history would be kind to today's leaders for bringing honor and self-pride to the expected 4 billion Africans that would inhabit planet earth by the end of this century. They would have to work to convince former colonial powers and the West that it would be in their interests to see a strong, united and democratic Africa.

They would finally have to let it be known to Africa's friends and foes that Africa will no longer allow itself to be exploited to maintain the wellbeing of others while simultaneously remaining underdeveloped. They would demand that Africa be treated with respect and would be open to make friends from both the East and West and anyone in between who would play by fair and equitable rules.

Another very bright development—the latest on the continent— is the recent Tripartite Free Trade Area, or what others prefer to call the Cape to Cairo Free Trade Corridor, which was launched on June 10, 2015 in Johannesburg, South Africa and due to go into effect in 2017. It was signed in the Egyptian seaside resort of Sham el-Sheikh on that same date and due to become effective in 2017.

This agreement will foster economic integration of the continent, given that it combines three major Economic Communities—namely the Common Market for Eastern and Southern Africa (COMESA), the East African Community (EAC), and the Southern African Development Community (SADC). This new, larger Free Trade Area brings 26 African Union member countries representing 48% of the AU membership and 51% of the continent's GDP with a combined population of 632 million.

As stated by Zodwa Mabuza and David Luke, expert negotiators for the TFTA and the United Nations Economic Commission for Africa, "If the Tripartite Free Trade Area were one country, it would be the thirteenth largest economy in the world." Trade in goods within this tripartite region grew from $2.002 billion in 2004 to $55 billion in 2012, representing an increase of 140% during this period.

The TFTA, formed independently of the AU institutional framework, will foster the ultimate goal of the African Union, which is to create a Continental Free Trade Area, expected to be launched in 2019. For its part, the TFTA is aimed in the first phase, and based on the three pillars of market integration, infrastructure development, and industrial development.

It should also be noted that the TFTA's goal is compatible with the objectives of the 1994 Abuja Treaty, which was specifically drawn up to create an African Common Market. Seen from this perspective, the TFTA is serving as a catalyst to the African Common Market, the Pan-African Continental Free Trade Area, and Customs Union.

While this book is not about the Tripartite Free Trade Area that spans half the continent with a GDP of 1 trillion USD, nor about its merits and demerits, it would nevertheless suffice to point out a few benefits that would accrue from this initiative.

Benefits

The very fact that leaders from the three regional African Economic Communities saw the need to foster economic integration among a diverse grouping of nation states is, in itself, a commendable development. Some of the obvious benefits would be increased trade among member states, which would divert trade from the rest of the world toward intra-TFTA trade. However, most importantly, gains to consumers would be enormous as they would get access to better quality and cheaper products.

Another noteworthy benefit would be the increase in industrial production, and diffusion of knowledge and best practices from more developed members. By harmonizing trade regime, operating costs would fall and Foreign Direct Investment flows into the region would increase. By speeding up economic growth through these measures, member countries would see the need to increase investment in infrastructure that would enable greater economic integration and stimulate further aggregate demand for goods and services.

Even though the bigger economies like South Africa's, Kenya, Egypt and Zimbabwe stand to benefit more, the spread factor would also benefit the smaller economies. Egypt's minister of trade and industry estimates that trade within the TFTA region would see a 25% increase over the next decade. Furthermore, streamlining clearance procedures for goods and reduction of customs fees should boost trade in merchandise and movements of people. The long-term goal is to reduce fees by 85% over the next three years.

Challenges

The enormous and multifaceted benefits notwithstanding, there exist a multiplicity of challenges that would have to be overcome before total integration of the TFTA member states is reached.

These challenges are first and foremost structural in nature. The fact that most African countries currently export significant quantities of their products to European Union member states and the USA while importing an equally large percentage of manufactured goods from outside the continent poses a stifling dilemma: how would diversification of manufactured goods be achieved?

Added to this situation is the unequal economic power of member states, with the more powerful expected to continue their dominance. As aforementioned, till this day, economic integration is still being seriously hampered by inadequate transportation infrastructure. This impedes trade in merchandise and movement of business persons, making transport costs prohibitively expensive and further slowing down trade. Transport costs in Africa remain the highest in the world. The proclivity of customs officials and other law enforcement elements to mount roadblocks and numerous controls further exacerbates these challenges.

According to French Radio RFI, the average time needed to clear goods through customs in Africa is one month compared to just ten days in Europe. The foot-dragging by some governments in eliminating customs duties at border crossings for fear of losing badly needed revenue is another challenge that would have to be addressed. Some scholars see the fact that resident foreign-owned but Africa-based transnational corporations with better technical know-how and greater financial outlays would be the bigger winners in the enlarged market.

In spite of the above challenges, I am of the opinion that in the long run, the benefits of regional, and eventually, continental economic union, would benefit almost everyone on the continent. Economies of scale and enlarged production capacities would spawn other rewarding economic activities, using information communication and technology to create more opportunities at all levels and categories of the population.

As is often said in business, those who are ready to sacrifice in the short-term would certainly reap huge sustained benefits in the long run. The short-term would pose serious problems for governments and their citizens, but it is important that their populations be educated and informed on the importance of this project in the long run.

In the meantime, the architects of the Pan-African common

market may need to look into creating temporary funding mechanisms for the lost revenue to some governments that are bound to result from open borders. These funds would cushion the shock and loss of state revenue that would normally go into social services and human investments.

As growth slows in China and Asia in general, opportunities open up in Africa. The declined demand for commodities from that region of the world frees up tremendous windows of opportunity for transformative industries in Africa. Manufacturing and investment in infrastructural assets would create jobs and spawn other attendant economic activities in the consumer sector.

At the end of the day, African countries and their governments could adopt the following entrepreneurship dictum: "Do what most people won't do for a few years, so that you will live the way most people can't for many years." Even though this statement is habitually applied to individuals and businesses, it could be expanded to underscore the need for whole nations and economic blocs as well. Simply stated, short-term pain and sacrifices will pay off and allow you to live very well for the rest of your life.

In closing, I would like to leave you the readers with this Chinese saying, "If you want to have prosperity for one year, plant or grow corn. If you want to have prosperity for ten years, grow trees. If you want to have prosperity for 100 years, grow people." As investment in education increases the literacy rate, the ever-resilient African people would understand the need to sacrifice in the short-term to have sustainable benefits in the long-term.

AFTERWORD

This book appropriately titled *Africa's Path to Economic Develop-ment: A Guide for Policy Makers and Scholars* is a culmination of many years of mulling and musings and encouragement from some intellectual friends. This work has been deliberately made short enough for target audiences but comprehensive enough to inter-est decision makers, students of economics, development studies, political science and development practitioners. It could serve the needs of high school students and beyond who aspire to a future in decision making in the public and private sectors, business and societal development. Finally, it would serve Pan-Africanists and those who believe Africa could do better given their richly endowed continent.

I have deliberately called out current African leaders and chal-lenged them to introspectively look themselves in the mirror and ask if their policies since independence, albeit the constraints of neo colonialism, have fostered or impeded the wellbeing of the governed. The answers to these perennial problems of underdevelopment, pov-erty and frustrations are equally a challenge to the next generation of leaders to chart a different course. It is my conviction that the future leaders would not roll over and let the continent's resources be continually exploited to the detriment of African peoples.

For a better Africa that its youths- its future would not con-tinue fleeing the continent to seek better livelihoods outside, and to enhance the chances of attaining the comprehensive goals of AGENDA 2063, the current leaders MUST create space at the decision-making tables for the millennials - the future of Africa across the continent. They must go beyond the empty slogans of how important the youths are, while effectively blocking meaningful participation of tomorrow's managers of modernization. Slogans must give way to concrete actions. Civil society organizations must be an integral player in the new Africa. Current leaders would have to consciously build strong national and continental institutions instead of strong men. Democracy and periodic change of leaders would be healthy for the continent while guarding against embracing the Western, especially American type democracy which is too expensive and lends the process to outside financing - itself a corrupting loophole. Economically, Africa's best path lies in the middle passage - a combination of the Washington Consensus and the Chinese model.

Finally, it is my hope that the other regions of the world would understand that it won't be business as usual with respect to their relationships with Africa where the causes and effects of underdevelopment would have to be eradicated. Mutually beneficial cooperative relations would become the new order replacing the old lopsided structure and system that has been in place since and preceding World War II and especially so since the late 1950s that has held the continent down and turned it into a laughing stock. Patience, education of the masses and understanding by the other international community actors would all be needed to move Africa toward the noble goals as enunciated and enshrined in the AGENDA 2063.

ENDNOTES

1 EY Emerging Markets Center of Excellence (2015); http://www.ey.com/gl/en/issues/driving-growth/emc-home

2 UN Stats on Corruption in Africa (2013); See https://www.transparency.org/cpi2013/results

3 The Wall Street Journal: The Modus Operandi. 10 December 1996 A1 by George Ayittey https://www.laits.utexas.edu/africa/ads/524.html

4 Jacob Rothschild on currency of a nation cited in Zeitgeist Addendum Documentary, quoting Senator Robert L Owen, Chair of Finance Committee on Banking and Currency during hearings that created the Federal Reserve Bank.

5 De Gaulle on Sovereignty; Martin, Garret Joseph (2015). *General de Gaulle's Cold War: Challenging American Hegemony*, 1963-68. Berghahn Books, Oxford.

6 Thomas Andersen and Carl-Johan Dalgaard, (2013). Power outages and economic growth in Africa, *Energy Economics*, 2013, vol. 38, issue C, 19-23; https://EconPapers.repec.org/RePEc:eee:eneeco:v:38:y:2013:i:c:p:19-23

7 http://www.enterprisesurveys.org, The World Bank.

8 https://www.oxfam.org/en/tags/corruption

9 https://www.uneca.org/publications/african-governance-report-iv

10 http://www.doingbusiness.org/rankings

11 One trillion dollar estimated to have left Africa for the West in last 30 years with $40 billion in 2010 alone through mispricing schemes by MNCs, https://www.oxfam.org/en/tags/trade-mispricing

12 University of Massachusetts Department of Economics. $500 billion via unfair trade rules.

13 The death of international development in http://blog.therules.org/essay-the-death-of-international-development/

14 35% more children needed teachers in 2012 than in 2000; http://uis.unesco.org/sites/default/files/documents/fs31-a-growing-number-of-children-and-adolescents-are-out-of-school-as-aid-fails-to-meet-the-mark-2015-en.pdf

15 The world's youngest continent will keep being run by its oldest leaders; https://qz.com/1162490/the-youngest-continent-keeps-on-being-run-by-the-oldest-leaders/

16 Bright, Jake & Aubrey Hruby, (2015). *The Next Africa: An Emerging Continent Becomes a Global Powerhouse*, Thomas Dunne Books, New York.

17 Educating Children in Poor Countries; https://www.imf.org/external/pubs/ft/issues/issues33/

18 Rawls, John. (1971). *A Theory of Justice*. Harvard University Press, Harvard.

19 The peoples' voice to challenge inequality; http://blog.therules.org/peoples-voice-challenge-inequality/

20 Stiglitz, Joseph E., (2013). *The Price of Inequality: How Today's Divided Society Endangers Our Future*. W. W. Norton & Company, London.

21 African diaspora remittances are better than foreign aid funds: diaspora-driven development in the 21st Century https://www.researchgate.net/publication/258338566_African_diaspora_remittances_are_better_than_

foreign_aid_funds_diaspora-driven_development_in_the_21st_Century

22 Mercer, Claire, Ben Page, and Martin Evans. 2008. *Development and the African Diaspora*. London: Zed Books.

23 Samba, Y., and Le Masson, O. 2005. Diaspora, développement et citoyenneté. Les migrants originaires du bassin du fleuve Sénégal (Mali, Mauritanie, Sénégal). URL: http://www.grdr.org/IMG/pdf/

24 Ollong, K A, (2013). Cameroonian Diaspora: An Assessment of its Role in Local Development, *Journal of Globalization Studies*, Vol. 4, 2; pp96-109.

25 One in eight people worldwide still chronically hungry, UN report finds; https://news.un.org/en/story/2013/10/451972-one-eight-people-worldwide-still-chronically-hungry-un-report-finds

26 Jason Miks, How Africa Could Feed the World cited in CNN-Global Public Square

27 Professor Emmanuel Nnadozie; Executive Secretary: Africa Capacity Building - African Union. Speech at New York University's Africa House -Investing in Africa's Human and Institutional Capacity. April 3, 2014.

28 Catherine KO, Economist Regional Integration is a Must for Africa at World Economic Forum. May 10, 2013.

29 Power People Planet: Seizing Africa's Energy and Climate Opportunities, Africa Progress Panel, June 10, 2015; http://cleancookstoves.org/resources/389.html

30 Kofi Anan, former UN Sec General and head of Africa Progress Panel cited in Africa Progress Report 2015. http://climateobserver.org/reports/africa-progress-report-2015/

31 Africa Climate Policy cited in 2015 Africa Progress Report; http://climateobserver.org/reports/africa-progress-report-2015/

32 Jesse Moore. Paris Climate Change Agreement - A Boom For LNG, A Bust for The Poor; December 16, 2015. https://seekingalpha.com/article/3760236-paris-climate-change-agreement-boom-lng-bust-poor

33 Simplice A. Asongu, *Project Syndicate: African Governance and Development Institute*; https://www.project-syndicate.org/columnist/simplice-asongu

34 B.R, Ambedkar Development Model of India: A Dalit Perspective. http://velivada.com/2017/07/20/development-model-india-dalit-perspective/

35 Le Schutter 2010: Assessing a Decade of Food Security and Rights to Food Progress; http://www.srfood.org/en/documents

36 Hannah Wittman, 2011, Food Sovereignty: A New Framework for Food and Nature; https://www.researchgate.net/publication/233698051_Food_Sovereignty_A_New_Rights_Framework_for_Food_and_Nature; Peter Rosset, 2009. Fixing our Global Food System: Food Sovereignty and Redistributive Land Reform; https://monthlyreview.org/2009/07/01/fixing-our-global-food-system-food-sovereignty-and-redistributive-land-reform/

37 Cotula, Lorenzo. (2013). *The Great African Land Grab?: Agricultural Investments and the Global Food System*. Zed Books, London.

38 See http://news.bbc.co.uk/2/hi/africa/4587584.stm

39 http://documents.worldbank.org/curated/en/179091468009576085/pdf/91
2070REVISED00ct20140vol100v120web.pdf

40 See https://softwarestrategiesblog.com/tag/cloud-computing-fore-
casts/

41 University of Michigan: William Davidson Institute citing World Bank
Report on Kenya's expected growth.

42 United Nations Economic Commission for Africa, and UNCTAD.

43 IMF World Economic Outlook 2016; https://www.imf.org/en/Publica-
tions/WEO/Issues/2016/12/31/Subdued-Demand-Symptoms-and-
Remedies

44 Generation 2030: Child Demographics in Africa; https://www.unicef.org/
publications/index_74751.html

45 UNICEF Report; Africa's Population Could Hit 4 Billion by 2100; https://
www.npr.org/sections/goatsandsoda/2014/08/13/340091377/unicef-
report-africas-population-could-hit-4-billion-by-2100

46 Optional Practical Training Extension for STEM Students; https://www.
uscis.gov/working-united-states/students-and-exchange-visitors/stu-
dents-and-employment/stem-opt

47 2016: When China Overtakes the US; https://www.theguardian.com/com-
mentisfree/cifamerica/2011/apr/27/china-imf-economy-2016

48 Tech Hubs in Africa: World Bank Group; http://blogs.worldbank.org/
ic4d/importance-mapping-tech-hubs-africa-and-beyond

INDEX

.